Students' Guide to Business Computing

Norman Stang and Frank Blewett

W0010033

Heinemann Newnes

Heinemann Newnes
An imprint of Heinemann Professional Publishing Ltd
Halley Court, Jordan Hill, Oxford OX2 8EJ

OXFORD   LONDON   MELBOURNE   AUCKLAND
SINGAPORE   IBADAN   NAIROBI   GABORONE   KINGSTON

First published 1989

British Library Cataloguing in Publication Data

Blewett, Frank
   Student's guide to business computing
   1.   Business firms. Applications of
   computer systems. System & analysis
   I. Title   II. Strang, Norman
   651.8

      ISBN 0-434-91877-6

Printed and bound in Great Britain by
Mackays of Chatham PLC, Chatham, Kent

Contents

Preface vii

1: The business enterprise 1
Objectives – the three main business sectors – organization within business – the hierarchy of personnel and responsibilities – the information needs of the business – business information systems

2: The business computer 24
Objectives – what is an information system – information processing – why are computers useful for a business – a simple computer–based information system – expertise needed to produce software – packages and tailored software – communication links – computing needs of a large business – organization structure of a large computer department – computing needs of a small business

3: Initiating the systems development life cycle 51
Objectives – the concept of systems – systems problems – the systems development life cycle – starting the systems development process – the preliminary investigation

4: Determination of system requirements 69
Objectives – organization charts – determination of requirements – developing a systems profile – fact-finding techniques – interviewing – structured and unstructured interviews – conducting an interview – fact-finding techniques – questionnaire – fact finding techniques – observation – fact-finding techniques – record inspection – determining user requirements – describing data elements

Contents

5: Systems design   99

Objectives – phases of systems design – design of the outputs from the system – major features of printed output and paper as a medium – design of computer input – the design of the data filing methods – file storage media – methods of file organization and processing – business databases – design of data controls and security systems – buying packaged software

6: Choosing and using a programming language   126

Objectives – what is a programming language – assembly languages – high–level languages – fourth generation languages (4GL) – development of programming expertise – database packages – expert systems

7: Applications software   149

Objectives – why use a computer for accounting – integrated accounting packages – stock control – purchase ledger – nominal ledger – payroll – interrelations between the accounting ledgers – contract accounting – fires, floods and other disasters – useful standard packages – other applications – specialist applications

8: Systems testing and implementation   185

Objectives – program and systems testing – the use of prototyping in systems development and testing – using 4GLs – training – changing over to the new system – file conversion – conversion to live files – estimating time requirements – bar charts – PERT charts

9: Selecting business computing hardware and software   208

Objectives – sizing the computer – assessing computer performance – IBM computers and compatibles – paying for the computer – selecting software – where can you buy computers – rules to follow in making a decision

Index   227

Preface

Computers, especially microcomputers, have become an everyday tool in all types of business ranging from one-man operations up to large international contractors. They have proved useful for a number of reasons, but a major reason is that computers can provide much better information than manual records. Accurate and immediate information is essential as a basis for good business planning and decision-making.

This book first discusses the requirements of a business for information, and then considers what computers can do to satisfy those needs. The major part of the book is concerned with defining systems requirements, and discussing the issues to be considered in designing a system.

Different possible approaches are considered such as programming a system from scratch, buying packaged software, or tailoring a package for your own requirements. We review briefly the different types of packaged software available, and also discuss various programming languages, including the current fourth generation languages (4GLs).

We then go on to discuss the issues to be considered in testing and implementing systems. Finally, we discuss the points to be considered in selecting business hardware and software, ending up with a summary list of DOs and DONTs.

The approach of the book is essentially practical, with tasks and assignments throughout so that the student actively learns. This book is suitable for college students taking a Business Studies or similar course leading to a BTEC National or Higher Level qualification, or an equivalent RSA or City & Guilds qualification. It is especially relevant to the HNC/HND Business Studies Option in *Business Information Technology*. It is also relevant to the ACCA Level 2 Unit in *Systems Analysis*, and to other similar units on professional accounting courses such as ACMA, ICSA, etc. It is also appropriate to various degree courses in Business and Accounting.

Computer software for use with this book

No specific software is required by this book, but students will gain considerable understanding if they have access to computers with relevant software. It is particularly useful to gain practical experience with commercial packages, especially accounting software such as *Pegasus* or *Sagesoft*. It is also very useful if students have gained some experience of programming with a database package such as dBASE4 (or dBASE3), Rbase or Paragon; alternatively, a minicomputer package such as Ingres or Informix will give them a useful understanding of fourth generation languages.

Frank Blewett and Norman Stang
The Business School
Polytechnic of North London

1: The business enterprise

Objectives

After reading this chapter, you should be able to:

- Explain what the purpose of business is
- Outline the functions of the various types of business sector in an economy
- Explain the major activities undertaken by business organizations.
- Describe how business is structured so as to enable their activities to be undertaken
- Describe what information is needed to support business structures, and how the information flows from one part of a business to another so as to create a business information system.

Scenario

Imagine you have just got a job in a burger bar. Your first task might be to clear away the litter from the tables and clean the floor. In this work you may feel remote from 'big business', yet, though you may be but a small cog in a large wheel, your task is sufficiently important to the burger bar to be worth employing you.

What is business?

Business can be said to be the activity of buying and selling products and services. The scenario presented would, on first appearance, appear to relate simply to the selling of burgers. However, this masks a long chain of business transactions; from farmers who rear the cattle, through to meat processors, and finally to the burger bar which cooks the processed meat. As to the trash which you are paid to clear away, here too you are part of a long chain of activities; from coal mining or oil extraction, through to the chemical processes which produce polystyrene cartons, and to the final waste disposal in large incinerators or municipal tips.

The purpose of business is to enable the final consumer of goods and services to satisfy his wants. As Adam Smith, one of the founding fathers of modern economic thought wrote over two hundred years ago 'The sole end of production is consumption.' In other words, there is no point in producing anything for which there is no consumer demand.

Of course, the consumer is not the only buyer of goods. The Government might decide to buy goods in bulk on behalf of individual consumers, medical supplies being a case in point; or for the nation as a whole, examples of this include defence or sponsorship of the arts.

Not all countries have the same methods of conducting business. In Britain, you, as an individual person are allowed to operate business activities. Or you may join other individuals in pooling your money and forming a company which will carry out business enterprise. The United States, Western European countries and Japan operate similar systems, known as *capitalist systems*. The Soviet Union and its allies, by contrast, do not normally allow individual persons or privately owned companies to conduct business affairs. Instead, the state, or country itself, owns the enterprises. This type of system is sometimes called a *socialist system* or a *state capitalist system*.

But, whatever the politico-economic system adopted by a country, the basic principles of business enterprise take in the activities of buying and selling. This normally requires that goods and services change hands in exchange for money.

The three main business sectors

We have already indicated that any job you might do would make you part of a large chain of business activities. For simplicity, we normally divide these activities into three main business sectors.

1 *The primary sector*: This is that part of the economy which is concerned with agriculture and fishing, and with mining and oil extraction. The primary sector is thus the starting-point in the business chain. Though this sector of the economy is no longer a

major employer, it nevertheless is important to the UK as we produce about half the food we consume as well as most of the coal and oil.

2 *The secondary sector*: This is often thought to be the most important part of the economy, accounting as it does for manufacture and construction. Thus all our factories, whether producing motor cars or baked beans, and our construction programmes, whether building houses or the Channel Tunnel, form part of the secondary sector. In recent years this has become less important as an employer, accounting for as few as one employed person in every four.

3 *The tertiary sector*: This is sometimes known as the *service sector* because it is concerned with providing services rather than with making things. Thus, the tertiary sector includes banking, insurance, retailing, travel, catering, and leisure pursuits. This sector of the economy employs as many as seven out of every ten workers.

So let us return to your job in the burger bar. Quite clearly, you are employed in the tertiary or service sector of the economy. The major feature of this sector is the direct contact between your company and its customers. Indeed, this might be highlighted by your work instructions such as always having to smile and be polite, and to quickly remove the litter left by previous customers so that new customers have a clean table at which to sit and eat their food.

The burger bar buys its food and packaging from the secondary sector, which is concerned with the manufacturing activities. The manufacturing companies, in turn, might buy from other manufacturers. Ultimately, though, manufacturers acquire their raw materials from the primary producers. These buying and selling chains are illustrated in Figure 1.1.

Questions

1 In the diagram on page 4 which business activities form part of which sectors?

2 What do all these businesses have in common?

3 Given that the burger bar also sells chips and requires oil for frying, can you extend the diagram to show the route by which these products become available?

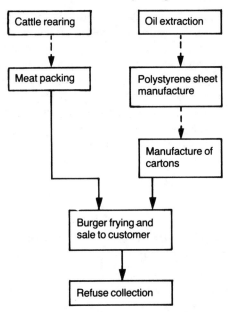

Figure 1.1   Buying and selling chains

In response to question 1, quite clearly cattle rearing and oil extraction are examples of primary sector activities. The handling of the meat and the manufacture of oil-based products are secondary sector activities; while the burger frying and waste disposal are tertiary activities.

But how did you deal with question 2? The chips originated as potatoes and the oil as a vegetable or vegetable seeds. These products are extracted from the ground as the result of farming activities. So, primary sector activities are involved. But what about the manu-facturing side of things? Well, the potatoes need to be graded, cleaned, peeled, and sliced into chips; the vegetable seeds are crushed and the oily liquid extracted and purified through filtration. So we do have other secondary sector activities involved in the preparation of food to be sold by our burger bar.

We have looked, so far, at business in general terms by focusing on one particular business. In doing so we have considered what a business is and how one business relates to another. Can we use this knowledge to answer question 3?

One approach we can use is simply to say that all businesses are involved in buying, making, and selling. This certainly appears to be true of all the businesses associated with the selling of burgers and chips. The farmer buys seed potatoes and works the soil in order to produce edible potatoes; a factory will buy the potatoes from the farmer and use machines to turn them into chips; the burger bar buys the raw chips, fries them, and sells them to the final customer.

Questions

4 Do all businesses buy, make and sell? Think of another business such as the bank in your local High Street.
5 What resources are needed by businesses?

We have looked at the activities leading up to the sale of burgers and chips. But how did you answer question 4? Let us start from the end. A bank sells services; for example, shopping would be somewhat more inconvenient if you had to use cash to pay for everything you bought. A bank allows you to pay for a pair of shoes through being able to hand over a cheque rather than cash. But what does the bank *make*? The bank is simply a transformation unit, converting your cheque into changes in two bank accounts, yours and the shoe shop's. The sum of money held in your account will fall by the value of the cheque, whilst that of the shoe shop will rise by the same amount. In other words, the bank *makes* bank account changes.

Finally, we can deal with the issue of what does the bank buy. In one sense it could be said to buy the use of your money while you are not using it. Suppose you receive a grant at the beginning of each term at college, and this is intended to last the entire term. If you pay the grant cheque into your bank acccount, the amount of money available for your use will rise by the value of the cheque. Any money in your account can be used by the bank, for example to lend to other customers. Thus the bank is using, or buying without necessarily paying you, your money.

The bank will also be buying other things. Compile a list of resources that a bank might need to use. This will help us answer question 5. The bank will need to have access to various resources. These can be categorized in several ways. For example as the 'three Ms':

1 *Men.* This is a generic term we sometimes use for human resources or labour. The bank will employ large numbers of people, some of whom you will see, such as the cashiers. There will also be many bank employees you will not see such as the computer staff and accountants.

2 *Money.* By this we mean financial resources, which could be cash or things which could easily be converted into cash should the need arise.

3 *Materials.* For a bank, the materials will include the building and its fixtures and fittings. It will also include computer equipment, weighing machines for bags of coins, paper, pens, etc.

An alternative way of looking at resources is to divide them into the three categories:

1 *Labour.* Very much the same as '*Men*' described above. Labour is a resource which can be changed in quantity fairly quickly. For example, the bank may increase the amount of labour services by having existing employees work extra hours, probably in return for an 'overtime' payment, or it may be able to recruit additional members of staff.

2 *Land.* By this we mean the plot of land on which the bank building stands, and the building itself. This is a resource which is generally fixed in supply over a fairly long period of time.

3 *Capital.* By capital we mean physical resources, some of which might have a relatively long life, such as computer equipment, and other resources which might last a short time such as paper. It would also include financial resources – money.

Organization within business

Business is interested in making the best possible use of the afore-mentioned resources. If the business firm's income from sales exceeds its expenditure on resources, then the firm is said to make a *profit*. In private enterprise, the business firm tries to earn as much profit as possible. A large part of the profit is normally handed over to the Government in the form of taxes, a smaller part is paid to shareholders, or investors in the company, as *dividends*. The remainder, often a greater sum than the total dividends, is kept by the business firm for future activities which, it hopes, would make the firm even larger and more profitable in the future.

Questions

6 List the tasks that need to be performed in a business such as a burger bar and draw a diagram which shows how the staff employed might be organized so as to make the best possible use of them.

7 Draw a diagram which shows how a bank's operations may be arranged in a departmental structure.

Let us return to our original scenario of a burger bar. Now answer question 6. Even in a small business such as this there are many different types of task to be performed. Here is a list we drew up:

● Checking on how much material (burgers, chips, etc.) are in stock
● Ordering the raw burgers, chips, etc
● Cooking the food
● Taking orders from customers and serving the goods
● Receiving payment from customers
● Clearing tables of litter and cleaning the floors
● Opening the burger bar in the morning and ensuring that it is locked at night
● Banking the money taken
● Paying the bills
● Answering the telephone and replying to letters
● Reconciling, or checking, the accounts
● Hiring and sacking staff
● Training the staff
● Supervision of staff.

This is a long list, and no doubt we have omitted some duties. Of course, not all the tasks need to be performed all the time. The burger bar needs to be opened only once each day, and the money may be paid into the bank only two or three times a week. This means that some member of staff may reasonably be expected to fulfil two or more responsibilities. On the other hand, it is unlikely that any employee will be expected to attempt to cook and serve customers at the same time.

A feature of modern business techniques is 'division of labour', that is splitting the jobs to be done between different people, who will often specialize in one aspect of the firm's operations.

In organizations larger than a simple burger bar, there normally will be a formal system of *departments*, with each department being responsible for one aspect of the operation. In some cases, a department may be further sub-divided into sections.

Consider the case of your local High Street bank in your answer to question 7. Perhaps the easiest approach you might use, other than asking at the bank, is to consider the types of transactions and processes in which the bank might be involved. These will include:

- Handling cash and cheques; receiving them from and paying them out to customers
- Opening new accounts and dealing with customers' problems
- Dealing with demands for foreign currency
- Lending money to customers
- Acting as a safe deposit for customers, allowing them to keep their valuables, such as jewellery and documents, in a safe deposit box.

These tasks would suggest that one approach might be to have a number of separate departments as follows:

1   A Cashier and Counter Department. The employees in this department would deal with everyday over-the-counter transactions such as taking deposits and paying out cash. They would also be responsible for the paperwork involved and ensuring that their cash tills have been properly managed.
2   A Customer Service Department whose personnel are concerned with dealing with matters beyond the scope of the cashiers. They would specialize in personal finance matters such as opening accounts and granting loans and even mortgages on houses and would also sell other banking services such as insurance.

3 A Foreign Exchange Department would have personnel who specialized in handling foreign currency matters. They would, for example, deal with customers who wanted to buy foreign currency or travellers' cheques; but their main work would be in the area of assisting companies which were exporting their products to other countries or importing goods from abroad.

These three departments would be able to handle all the banking functions previously mentioned and are concerned with the bank's role as a buyer and seller. However, there are some internal administrative matters which require separate departments. So we can extend our list of departments to include:

4 A Personnel Department which is concerned with all matters regarding the bank's employees. This department may be composed of separate specialist sections, each dealing with one of the following functions:
● recruitment and dismissal of staff and the keeping of appropriate records
● staff training.

5 A Salaries Department, responsible for calculation of employees' pay, including sick pay and holiday pay entitlement.

6 An Audit Department whose staff check that the various branches of the bank are keeping their books correctly and that there are no financial irregularities.

7 A Finance Department, responsible for checking the bills sent to the bank by their suppliers and then paying those bills.

8 An Estate and Premises Department which has staff responsible for the upkeep of the property owned by the bank.

9 A Computer Department, staffed with systems analysts, programmers, operators and data entry personnel. These employees are concerned with the smooth functioning of the computer procedures.

It is quite likely that these last six departments will be found mainly at the bank's head office, because these are often regarded as 'central' functions. It is likely, however, that the branch will also employ personnel with local responsibilities in those areas.

The hierarchy of personnel and responsibilities

Let us return once again to our burger bar and consider your position in the company. There you are busily cleaning the tables, but who decides that you do this work and who decides which tables to clean? Who do you turn to if you have any work problem? To answer those questions we need to ask 'who is in charge?'

But let us first consider another question, namely 'what does the person who is in charge actually do?' Well, to answer that we might draw up a list of things that might be done by the person in charge. Such a list for the burger bar might include the following:

1 Hiring and firing of staff.
2 Ensuring that enough burgers, chips, etc. are available for frying and selling to customers.
3 Dealing with customers' complaints.
4 Making decisions that cannot be made by other members of staff.

So, to answer the original question, the person who is in charge of the burger bar is the individual who carries out the tasks listed above. He or she is likely to be called the *manager*, and the other employees are known as *subordinates*. If our burger bar is one of a chain of similar establishments, then each bar will have its own manager, each of whom will be a subordinate to a more senior manager, perhaps an operations manager who will be located at the company's head office.

Also at the head office of our chain of burger bars will be located various central departments, similar to those of our High Street bank. These will include a finance department, a personnel department, a computer department, etc., each headed by a manager. Each of these managers is responsible for the proper running of his or her own department and may not interfere in the running of another manager's department.

In turn, groups of senior managers will report to a *director* of the company. Unlike a manager, a director is not normally concerned with the day-to-day running of any department; instead a director is concerned with problems which the company might face in the future. And it is at a meeting of the board of directors that the major decisions governing the company are made.

Questions

8 List the positions and nature of responsibility at each level in a business.
9 Draw a diagram showing the hierarchy of responsibilities in a bank.

In this section we have worked up the personnel hierarchy of our burger bar business, from you to the directors of the company. But to answer question 8, let us look formally at the personnel hierarchy, but this time working down from the top and looking at the type and level of responsibility associated with each person.

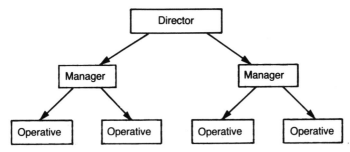

Figure 1.2   The personnel hierarchy

- The *Director* is concerned with *strategic* matters, that is, how the business is to face the future. Decisions at this level are concerned with overall broad policy concerning the company as a whole
- The *Manager* is involved in *tactical* matters, that is, carrying out policy laid down by directors. Decisions are made only in relation to *how* the department will implement company policy
- The *Operative* is employed to perform a task or job of work and normally does not make decisions of great importance. What decisions are made at this level might be how best to perform the task.

The information needs of the business

All organizations need a constant flow of timely information if they are to operate efficiently. This information will relate to the resources that the organization needs to use – men, money and materials.

11

Questions

10 List the types of information that might need to flow from one part of the burger bar operation to another.
11 List the types of information that might need to flow between the burger bar and the head office.
12 What are the differences between the two information lists produced in response to questions 10 and 11?

To answer question 10 you will need to bear in mind that the individual burger bar is concerned only with its own needs. What does your list look like?

In producing our list, we looked back to our answer to question 6. We found that it was possible to look at the tasks and first eliminate those which did not involve any major flow of information from one part of the burger bar operation to another. This left us with the following list:

1   Taking orders from customers and serving the goods.
2   Receiving payment from customers.
3   Answering the telephone and replying to letters.
4   Hiring and sacking staff.

We can take this list and re-arrange it so that the tasks relate to the three major resources of:

1   *Personnel*.
    ● This gives us hiring and sacking staff
2   *Materials*.
    ● This provides us with taking orders from customers and serving the goods
3   *Money*.
    ● This gives us a further list comprising receiving payment from customers
4   We can add the fourth type of information, namely:
    ● answering the telephone and replying to letters.

In terms of sheer volume, most of the information will take the form of verbal information (a spoken request for food) and the exchange of money for the food. This information-passing is purely local, the burger bar being a self-contained unit, and is simply concerned with the function of serving the customer. In other words, it is 'operational' by nature.

Now look at your list in response to question 11. This will be different, but again we can divide the topics into resource areas as follows:

1 *Personnel*. The manager will pass information to head office about new members of staff and leavers and about the hours worked by employees. In return, head office will update their files, calculate pay, and send the relevant pay information to the burger bar.

2 *Materials*. The manager will check supplies of raw food and other goods and will complete a form requesting additional supplies. In return, head office will send the required goods together with confirmation documentation.

3 *Money*. The manager will need to inform head office regularly about how much money has been earned from sales to customers. It is quite likely that head office will inform the manager of the burger bar's financial performance relative to targets set by head office; this will be based upon money earned from sales and the cost of supplying the service.

This information, which passes between the burger bar manager and head office, does not contain the details of each individual sale. After all, head office is not interested in the fact that the Ongar family bought eight hamburgers, nine portions of chips, two lemonades and six strawberry milkshakes; nor is it interested in the fact that the bill came to £13.10. What head office needs to know is how many burgers, portions of chips, and so on, were sold in total during the course of the week and how much money was paid by all its customers during the same period of time.

This information could be described as tactical, showing how the burger bar carried out its task, namely to earn money by selling hamburgers and other fast food products. The information, when collected for each unit in the burger bar chain, can then be used for strategic planning, where the directors examine trends in sales and decide on future policy.

Business information systems

Now let us consider how the head office of the burger bar chain might handle the information it receives. The business needs to ensure that it has *all* the *relevant* information to hand *when it needs it*. In later chapters of this book we will be examining various methods that might be adopted to achieve this. For the moment, though, we will concentrate on the *business operations requirements* of the firm.

Questions

13 List the sources of the various inflows and outflows of money and show how a company might distinguish between the different uses of its money and how it keeps track of its various financial commitments.
14 What information is required in relation to employees of the company?
15 How does a company deal with the stock requirements of its branches?

Our burger bar business finds that money flows into and out of the company virtually every day of the year. Question 13 asks you to list the places where the money comes from and where it goes to. Let us begin with where the money comes from. This should be easy. The main source of income will be from customers who buy hamburgers, chips, and other fast foods. There may be other sources of income. For example, the company may own property which it rents out to some other business organization or it might earn some money from a television or film company for allowing filming to take place on its premises; the possibilities are almost endless. But whatever the source of income, the company must keep precise records of receipts of money, showing how much was received from whom and when it was received.

Now let us consider the other list, that of where the money goes to. Our list would include:

1 Suppliers of basic, raw foodstuffs.
2 Suppliers of packaging.
3 British Telecom for the use of telephones.

4   Various local councils in whose areas the company has property.
5   Suppliers of gas, electricity and any other fuel.
6   Suppliers of office equipment, stationery, etc.
7   Advertising and other promotional expenses.
8   Professional fees paid to auditors, solicitors, etc.
9   Wages and salaries paid to employees.
10 Inland Revenue and HM Customs and Excise for tax which is owing.

Perhaps you can add items to our list. But as you can see there are many people and organizations to whom money is paid. These payments must be recorded in precise detail. This will include the name and address of the person or organization receiving the money, how much money and when it was paid. Before the days of computing equipment, all such business transactions were recorded by hand in books known as *ledgers*. Details of income were recorded in the *sales ledger* and details of outflows of money were recorded in the *purchase ledger*. These titles are still used in computer-based systems to denote these traditional differentiations between income and expenditure. We will have more to say about these in Chapter 7.

But do note that at least one of the items on our list does not feature on the purchase ledger. This is the payment of wages and salaries to employees which is controlled through a separate system known as the *payroll*.

Question 14 asked you to list the information required to be held in such a system. Without wishing to go into great detail, we can say that this must show for each payment period such details as *how much* was paid and the *basis* for such payment, and how much was deducted for *tax, national insurance, pension scheme, etc.* Relevant parts of this information will be used to calculate how much should be in each employee's pay packet; other parts will be required by the tax authorities.

We can analyse the sales and purchase ledgers and the payroll to see how the company has performed financially over a given period of time. The accountants may wish to see which elements of financial details are giving rise to concern for the future well-being of the company and may therefore have to be restrained.

At the end of the year the accountants will want to provide information about the overall financial performance of the company. They will publish tables known as the *profit and loss account* and the

15

balance sheet which are intended to show the company's financial performance over the year and its current financial standing. Such information might be used by the financial press and possible investors to judge whether the company was doing as well as expected and whether it was worth investing further funds in the company. To do this, it will be necessary to merge information relating to all the flows of money into yet another ledger known as the *nominal ledger* or *general ledger*.

The relationships between these various systems is shown in the diagram below:

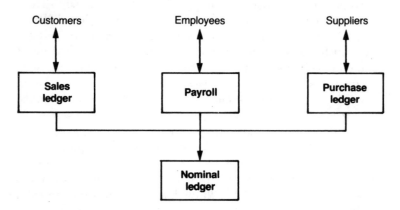

Figure 1.3   Relationships between the various systems

Another major area of concern to the company is the recording of stock transactions. The company needs to consider not only the stock requirements of its branches, but also the overall stock position as it pertains to its central warehouse. Let us begin by considering how the company deals with the requirements of each burger bar.

Question 15 asked you to detail how you would organize this. There are many ways open to you. We would suggest the following at the very least. There must be some procedure laid down whereby the manager can order supplies from the central warehouse and have the goods delivered in good time to meet the burger bar's needs. This requires that the following stages be followed:

1   It is determined that there is going to be a shortage of supply of some product in the near future unless stock is replenished. The

manager is probably in the best position to check how much is in stock at the burger bar and compare this amount with how much is expected to be required for the following few days.

2 The need for additional supplies needs to be communicated to head office. This could be done over the telephone, by post, or through some electronic mail system. It is likely that some standard form will be used to notify head office of the requirement. But whatever method is used, it is important that head office understands how much and of what product is required.

3 The goods need to be delivered from the warehouse to the burger bar. This, in turn, will require that some documentation is produced to instruct the warehouse what to send, with a copy being sent with the goods so that the burger bar manager can check that the correct goods have been received.

What we have looked at is the stock system as it affects the burger bar manager. Of course, the overall procedure has a much wider effect. It seems rather obvious to take some of the following factors into consideration:

1 There must be some procedure to ensure that the burger bar manager's request is checked for correctness and reasonableness. For example, the company must check that the manager has not ordered something that the company does not supply. Similarly, it must check that the manager has not asked for an absurd quantity such as one thousand cases of burger buns when the burger bar uses an average of one hundred cases a week.

2 There must be some means of checking that the quantity of goods requested is in fact available in the warehouse. After all, it is possible that the warehouse will at some time run short of some item.

3 If the central warehouse is running short of a product there must be some procedure laid down to ensure that the product is re-ordered from the supplier.

4 There must be a procedure to handle goods being received into the warehouse from suppliers and the updating of the file containing information about stock availability. It would be illogical to have the system refuse to supply a product simply because the computer records have not caught up with reality.

5 Finally, there must be some system which enables the warehouse employees to know what is to be packed and shipped to each burger bar.

Most businesses have formal or set procedures which employees are expected to follow. Many of the procedures mentioned above could be carried out without using computers; and we should remember that not all businesses use computers in their accounting and stock control procedures. The benefit of modern computer systems lies in their use in attempting to integrate these activities to produce a single, coherent system which allows appropriate staff access to information that they need to use.

Larger businesses may perform a wide variety of operations and the resulting systems will therefore be more extensive and complex. For example, a large motor car manufacturer may have, in addition to the ledger, payroll and stock control requirements mentioned above, the following systems:

1 *Sales Order Processing*. This is a system which enables the company to accept specific orders from the customer for a particular model of motor car with a specified engine size, colour of paintwork and level of body trim.
2 *Production Control*. This is a system designed to follow the order through the entire manufacturing process. This ensures that the workers on the production line know what engine to fit, what colour paint to use, what type of radio to install, etc. This system is further linked to the stock control system to ensure that the required components are available where and when they are needed.

Assignment 1

Select a local business and for that business:
(a) List the various separate business functions that need to be performed.
(b) Draw a diagram which shows:
    (i) how these different functions relate to one another and,
    (ii) the flow of information between the functions.

Recap

A *business* is concerned with buying, making and selling.
The main business sectors are:
1 The *primary sector* which is concerned with agriculture, fishery, and mineral extraction.
2 The *secondary sector* in which is found manufacturing and construction.
3 The *tertiary sector* which comprises of the services such as banking, transport and leisure.

Business uses resources comprising of *people, money* and *materials*. Business carries out its functions through *division of labour*, whereby people are normally put into separate specialist departments. Each department has a person in charge, known as the *manager*, and groups of managers often report to an even more senior member of staff. The more senior the member of staff, the wider the interests, such that a director will be concerned with the future 'well-being' and direction of the company, whereas the operative or shop-floor worker will be concerned with performing a narrowly defined task.

A *business information system* is concerned with ensuring that up-to-date information is available when necessary to appropriate members of staff.

The business information system usually comprises of a series of interlocking functional systems concerned with accounting for the resources of people, money and materials.

Answers

1 Primary sector – cattle rearing and oil extraction. Secondary sector – meat packing, polystyrene sheet manufacture, cartons manufacture. Tertiary sector – burger frying and sales, refuse collection.
2 All the businesses are concerned with buying inputs (known as *factors of production*), of a certain value, doing something with those factors of production, and selling the output so as to make a financial profit.

3

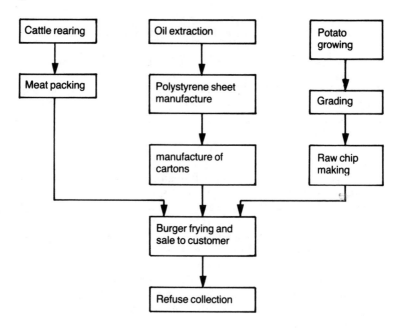

4 In one sense they do. Even a bank buys something – the labour services of its employees – and sells it to customers.

5 The resources needed by businesses go under a number of headings including:

men, money, materials

labour, land and capital

6 Checking stocks of raw materials – ordering raw materials if required – drawing materials from the refrigerator/freezer – cooking – taking orders from customers and serving the food – receiving payment for the food – cleaning – opening up and closing the premises – taking money to the bank – paying bills – dealing with letters, telephone calls – checking accounts – staffing, i.e. hiring, training, supervising.

7 At branch level:

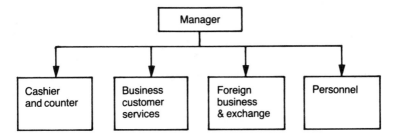

8 Director – overall responsibility for the company or a major functional area of the company's operations. Concerned with strategic matters.

Manager – responsible for tactical matters, carrying out company policy in so far as it affects his department. Supervisory role.

Operative – shopfloor worker or office clerk, carries out the day-to-day operations.

9

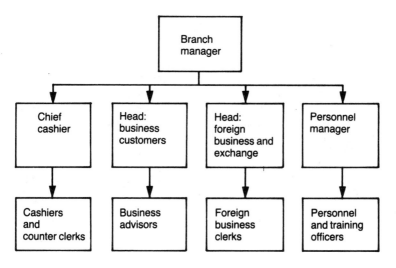

10 Stock information– shortages, damage
   Orders from customers
   General supervisory instructions
   Cash information
   Work hours schedules

21

11 Stock information – replenishment orders
   Bills received
   Information on takings banked
   Information on new employees and leavers

12 The list in question 10 is essentially local, likely to be spoken or written on paper. The list in question 11 tends to be wider by nature and is used for company-wide planning; much of the information ends up in a computer-based system.

13 Inflows of money – mainly from customers who pay for the goods and services they buy, possibly from property they rent out; there will also be an inflow of money if the company raises a loan with their bank.

Outflow of money – most goes to pay bills including wages, raw materials, telephone, gas and electricity, office supplies, rental of property, rates, taxes, advertising agencies, auditors and solicitors.

To keep track of financial commitments, a company will use ledgers, whether paper or electronic. A sales ledger will hold information about money owing to the company; a purchase ledger will contain the information about how much the company owes, to whom, and from when. The information from these two ledgers feeds into a nominal ledger in which the money values associated with the various transactions are placed into separate accounts known as nominal codes.

Accountants are employed to devise ways of showing how the money is used. A common method is to assign groups of nominal code numbers on the basis of sales, employment costs, materials costs, and overheads with each code number having a specific purpose and having an annual budget allocated to it. The groups of nominal codes can be analysed and compared with the budget.

14 The first point to note is that precise legal requirements for tax and national insurance change over time. Generally, each employee must have a unique identification number (or works number) and there are two types of information required. First, information of a personal nature such as name, address, date of birth, and national insurance number. Secondly, information that will be needed for the calculation of the employee's pay, tax and other deductions. This will include the rate of pay, tax code number, national insurance code, and information on gross pay, tax and national insurance paid so far in the current tax year.

A mixture of personal and pay information is produced each year and copies sent to the individual employee and to the tax office.

15 There must be procedures to deal with:
- Determining that there are, or will soon be, shortages
- Sending orders for fresh supplies to head office
- Deliveries to the branches.

2 : The business computer

Objectives

After reading this chapter, you should be able to:
- Understand the nature of an information system, and appreciate why good information systems are important
- Explain why computers are useful for a business
- Describe the distinction between 'packaged' software, 'tailored' software and 'bespoke' software, and be able to see where these different types of software are appropriate.
- Outline the computing needs of a large business, and the structure of a large computer department.
- Outline the computing needs of a typical small business.

Scenario

Imagine you are working in a burger bar, as in Chapter 1, and you have to take over running things, because the manager is going to be away ill for a month. You may feel that a computer is not much use in frying burgers or seeing that customers are served, but this is a very short-term perspective. If you want to know how much to pay staff, or what food to order from suppliers, or if you want to find out how much profit the burger bar is making, then a computer can be very useful to you in setting up a good information system.

What is an information system?

Let us think again about the problems of running a burger bar. Suppose that a supplier rings you up and asks you if you want to order more mustard and tomato ketchup. How do you decide? You need to consider:

- customer demand, i.e. how quickly are they used up?
- current stocks, i.e. how much is there left?

One way of checking current stocks is to go to the stock cupboard and count what is there. This may be satisfactory for a small business, but in a larger business, such actual counting is far too slow and time-consuming. Imagine the supplier still at the end of a telephone while you go down to the stock cupboard and do a careful count!

A better approach is to set up an *information system*, to record what you have in stock; this does not require a computer, although often it may be more effective to use one. For the burger bar, an information system could consist of just a set of cards, one for each item in stock (burgers, buns, sachets of ketchup, etc.). The card would typically record the cost price at which the item is purchased from the supplier, and how much of it is currently in stock. This would then enable you to find out immediately what was in stock at any time without going down to the stock cupboard. A sample record card for this system is shown in Figure 2.1.

Burger Bar LTD				Stock Card	
Item description Tomato Ketchup		*Supplier*	Musgrove Wholesalers Ltd., 23 Whiting Road, Harlow, Essex.		
Pack size 100 sachets		*Contact*	Bill Jones 0279 - 10075		
Cost price £1.10					
Stock changes Opening quantity: 50 packs					
	Date	*Amount delivered*	*Amount issued*	*Closing quantity*	*Comments*
	27/5		10	40	
	5/6		20	20	75 ordered 6/6
	10/6	75		95	
	17/6		10	85	

Figure 2.1   Sample stock record card

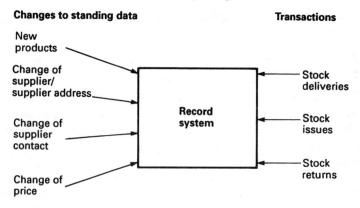

Figure 2.2   Updates to stock record system

The only difficulty with such a system is that it needs to be kept accurately, by *updating* it every time a change is made. Figure 2.2 shows some of the regular updates which might need to be made to this system in order to keep it accurate; each change to the system is referred to as a *transaction*. A stock system such as this can have many transactions, and entering these changes each time can be very time-consuming. Often, businesses decide that it is not worth entering every single operation into the system; they compromise by keeping stock records in large units. Thus, the chef might have to sign a chit each time they open a pack of 100 burgers, or a box of 200 sachets of tomato ketchup. The stock records would then only refer to complete packs, or boxes, or whatever other large unit was appropriate.

The key point to remember with any information system is that 'time is money'. Even this simple system has two significant costs associated with it:

● *Set-up costs*: someone has to spend time designing the stock cards and filling them in when the system is set up
● *Running costs*: time is spent updating the cards each time a new transaction is entered.

Such costs are often ignored, because the time involved is just a few minutes now and then. However, this may be a mistake, because it can still add up to quite a few hours over a week, costing substantial sums.

Why bother with all this paperwork, then? There are two very strong reasons for doing so:

- *Better management information*
- *Better financial control*.

To understand why good management information is useful, think again of taking over running the burger bar when the manager has fallen ill. How do you decide what to order from suppliers, or what invoices need to be paid? Without any records, you will not have a clue; all knowledge of the business will be in the manager's head. With a reasonable information system, it is relatively easy to discover what is currently in stock and how much of it has been used in the last few weeks . . . you can then decide easily how much ought to be ordered.

As we shall discover later, especially where an information system is kept on a computer, there can be many other benefits for management decision-making.

The advantages of good financial control may be less obvious to you, but they are just as important. A major problem in stock control is what is known as *shrinkage*, or loss of stocks. Shrinkage can happen because of deterioration of food e.g. buns go stale, or burgers become too old to be used. However, the main reason for shrinkage is theft by staff; stealing food to eat at home, or more likely stealing large packets of burgers to sell off profitably elsewhere. A good information system together with a tightly controlled store cupboard can ensure a low level of shrinkage. Without any such record, you will not even know how much has been lost.

Questions

1 As manager of the burger bar, you are also responsible for ensuring that suppliers are correctly paid, exactly twenty-eight days after invoicing you. If you were designing a payments system, what information would need to be recorded on each record card referring to an individual supplier?

2 Draw a diagram showing all the various updates that would have to be made to this payment system.

3 Why could a computer be useful to the burger bar for its stock records and payments systems?

Information processing

Our answer to the first question would be to have a large card, with relatively fixed information (name, address, contact name, telephone number) at the top, and a large number of lines below for information about individual invoices. A possible design is shown in Figure 2.3. Notice that the data on a record is precisely defined by the objectives of the system: in this case, the objectives are simply to record details of invoices, and to ensure that suppliers are paid after twenty-eight days. The basic rule with updating is that everything on the record may change at some stage; the main updates are shown in Figure 2.4. Regular updates, such as entering invoices and payments, will be added to the record card. More unusual changes, such as a change of the supplier's address, may require a new record card, because there is no space on the card.

However, the system as it stands is not adequate. As the manager, how do you decide what invoices need to be paid each day? The only way of determining this is to look through all the cards: a time-consuming process where some invoices will get overlooked, even though they are due for payment. Some more efficient reminder system is needed; the obvious way of dealing with this is to file the invoices in date sequence, and simply look first at the invoice file each day to find which invoices are due for payment.

Thus, an information system needs to be designed so that data can be easily *captured*: both the initial data and updates. It also needs to be designed so that information can readily be *retrieved*.

Why could a computer be useful to the burger bar?

The obvious reason is to save costs, because the time spent updating a computer system is likely to be less than with a manual record system. This is important, but may not be the main reason why it is worth using a computer. In fact, the major reasons are usually those already mentioned as a justification for setting up an information system, namely *better management control* and *better management information*.

A manual records system often tends to consist of numerous pieces of paper, with records that are haphazardly updated, and not greatly trusted as a source of information. Computer systems tend to impose a much greater discipline on staff: staff need to be more carefully trained in order to use computer systems, because it is easy to make a

Burger Bar Ltd				Purchase Ledger Card	
Supplier Musgrove Wholesalers Ltd., 23 Whiting Road, Harlow, Essex.				*Contact* Bill Jones 0279 – 10075	
Initial balance owing: £110.75					
Invoice no.	*Date received*	*Amount*	*Date paid*	*Closing balance*	
100573	26/5	£57.25		£168.00	
100325		£110.75	4/6	£57.25	
100573		£57.25	22/6	£0.00	
100931	30/6	£85.45		£85.45	

Figure 2.3   Payments record card

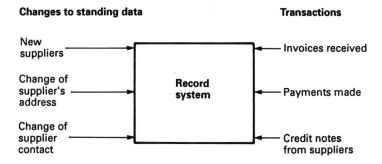

Figure 2.4   Updates to payment records

mess of entering data into a computer. However, because of this stricter discipline, the information in a computer system is likely to be much more up-to-date and accurate than in a manual information system.

The quality of information from a computer system is clearly a great advantage. For example, it is possible at any time to print a list of suppliers, together with amounts owing to them. Alternatively, you can print out a list each day of what invoices are due to be paid or even get the computer to print out the cheques to pay the suppliers. Similarly, from a computerized stock system, it is possible to print out weekly or monthly summaries showing how much has been used of different stock items; this is useful, if you want to know how much to order. Extracting the same summaries from a manual record system will involve considerable time and effort.

What we have not considered here is whether it is worth buying a computer for the burger bar. To do this, we should need to consider all the costs involved and we have only considered the benefits so far. We shall come back to the question of costs later; any feasibility study for computerization must consider this. For the time being, we want to concentrate on why businesses use computers, before considering why it is not always such a good idea.

Why are computers useful for a business?

People often think of computers as being devices which can perform very complicated calculations much faster than human beings can. This is certainly true, and businesses often use computers to solve complex mathematical equations in a few seconds, which otherwise might take weeks to solve. For example, a large oil company such as Shell has to collect crude oil from hundreds of oil wells all over the world. This needs to be delivered by oil tankers to numerous refineries in the quantities required by them, and tankers need to be allocated to refineries in such a way as to minimize the total transport costs. The solution of this complex problem can take several hours each week, even on the largest modern computer. Without a computer, money would be wasted because ships would travel further than they needed to, and refineries would often not have the crude oil that they needed.

Many other uses of computers by businesses can be identified. Computers can be used to draw graphs or charts of sales for different products. They can be used by car designers to find the right shape for car bodies and by architects to design buildings; this is known as *computer-aided design (CAD)*. They can also be used to control operations in a fully automated factory; this is known as *computer-aided manufacture (CAM)*.

However, for most businesses, the major need is to have effective information systems. The vast majority of current applications of computers by businesses are concerned with the provision of information, and that is what this book is about.

Other books in this series have described computer hardware and software, and you should refer to the reading-list if you know little about computers, as we shall not repeat the same basic knowledge here. The following questions are a useful reminder of some points that you ought to know about computers.

Question

4 List the major hardware parts of a modern computer, and explain why they are important for processing a business information system on a computer.

Hardware

In answering question 4, the most important parts of a computer, which make it particularly useful for storing business information systems, are:

- *Processor* which controls all operations of the computer, and performs calculations. The processor operates according to a defined set of complex instructions, known as a *computer program* (or *software*)
- *Memory* which provides immediate, temporary storage for programs and data currently being processed. Accessible memory is known as RAM (random access memory), while ROM (read-only memory) is used to store the program which starts up the computer
- *Screen* and *keyboard* which enable the user to interrogate the computer or type in data, as well as receiving information from the computer
- *Printer* which outputs results from the computer in printed form, often referred to as 'hard copy'
- *Magnetic disk* which is used for permanent storage of computer software and data files, which may include very large data files, containing tens of thousands of individual data records.

Microcomputers have developed rapidly since they were first introduced in the late 1970s, but the key hardware development in supporting business information systems has been the introduction of cheap, fast high-capacity disks. Even very cheap business micros now have hard disks which can store 20 MB (1 MB = 1 megabyte, or one million characters); larger computers have disks which can hold hundreds or even thousands of megabytes. The simple system for the burger bar may not require megabytes of disk space, but there are many businesses that do.

For example, a relatively small business selling goods on credit may have 10,000 customers; for each customer, they need to keep names and addresses, and details of what payments are outstanding from that customer, as well as other important information. This can easily require as much as 500 characters per customer, or a total of 500 × 10,000 = 5 MB. Remember also that this is only one data file, and the business is likely to have many other files that must be kept.

Questions

5 Assume the payments system for the burger bar is run on a micro-computer. The computer needs to be able to print out the names and addresses of suppliers, together with details of the amount currently owing, and amounts paid to the supplier over each of the last three months. Design a suitable data file to store this data on disk. Assuming the bar has fifty different suppliers, how much disk space would be needed for the supplier file?

6 For the information system in question 5, list as many tasks as you can, which will need to be carried out by the computer in order to keep records up-to-date and to produce the information that the burger bar requires.

A simple computer-based information system

We have said already that the design of an information system should be dictated by the objectives of the system, i.e. what it is expected to do. For question 5, it is simply necessary to ensure that all the required information is contained in the data file, and that each *field* (or data item) is allocated enough space on the disk. A suitable design would be like the design shown on p 33.

Field	Format	Bytes	A sample record
Supplier reference	XXXXXXXX	8	ARBUTSJO
Supplier name	X(25)	25	Arbutson Jones Ltd
Supplier address 1	X(25)	25	125, Handsworth Rd
Supplier address 2	X(25)	25	Teddington
Supplier address 3	X(25)	25	Middlesex
Post code	X(8)	8	TW12 8PJ
Total amount owing	999999.99	9	002305.45
Amounts paid –			
2–3 months ago	999999.99	9	002000.21
1–2 months ago	999999.99	9	001822.00
0–1 month ago	999999.99	9	000750.75

TOTAL 152 bytes

The notation used above is that X represents one character (letter, comma, number, etc.); thus X(25) is a field which holds up to 25 characters. A numeric digit is represented by 9; thus, 999999.99 represents a field which can only hold numeric data, with 6 digits before the decimal point and 2 digits after, i.e. this field can hold monetary amounts of anything less than £1,000,000.

Notice that arbitrary decisions have to be made on the maximum size of fields. Here, the name and address is limited to twenty-five characters per line, although often, slightly more space may be required; similarly, a decision has to be made as to the largest monetary amounts that may be encountered for an individual supplier.

This system would be of little use if you wanted to keep track of particular invoices, and whether they had been paid. To provide this information, you would need to keep more data on disk relating to individual invoices.

The disk requirements for this file would not be very great: 50 suppliers × 152 bytes = 7600 bytes. In practice, it would be necessary to index records, and the index file might add an overhead of 50% or so i.e. another 3800 bytes, making a total of 11,400 bytes. Even so, the total disk requirement will be no more than about 11 or 12K, compared to a hard disk which holds at least 20 megabytes.

Updating the system

Regarding question 6, the advantage of a simple design such as this is that it needs relatively little updating.

The main tasks are shown in the table below.

Task	*Effect on file*
Enter new supplier details	Create new record
Enter new supplier address	Update record
Enter amount for new invoice	Update amount owing
Enter total amount paid	Update amount paid (0–1 month)
Run end-of-month routine	Move amount (1–2 month) to (2–3)
	Move amount (0–1 month) to (1–2)
	Zero amount for 0–1 month

So far, we have simply considered what tasks need to be performed by a computer in order to process an information system. We need now to discuss how a computer can most economically be programmed to carry out such tasks.

Software

Software consists simply of computer programs: a program is a set of instructions, usually stored on magnetic disk, to tell a computer how to carry out particular tasks. These programs may have been specially written, or may have been bought, ready written to perform that task. A convenient classification is as follows:

1 *Systems software*: the software usually purchased with computers. This includes the operating system (to control operations of the computer) together with other essential routines (e.g. to copy disks, or to tell you how much space is left on a disk).
2 *Utility software*: this is purchased separately from the operating system, but performs tasks fairly similar to systems software. Examples are programs to sort large data files very quickly, or disk cacheing software which speeds up processing by writing printer output into RAM (random access memory) prior to printing.
3 *Standard packages*: these meet very standard requirements which apply to most users. Examples are word processing, spreadsheets, and database software. The best-known packages have sold millions of copies.

4   *Applications software*: this is specifically designed to cárry out a set of tasks directly relevant to the operations of a business. Such software may be purchased as a 'ready-written' package, or may be written especially for the user.

The first three types of software are usually purchased directly from computer dealers or software houses. We assume that you will already have some knowledge of what software is, and how an operating system works. The best-known operating systems are probably MS-DOS (on IBM-compatible microcomputers), Microsoft OS/2 on IBM PS/2 microcomputers, and UNIX which runs on a wide range of multi-user systems. Larger computers tend to have their own proprietary operating systems, and often different models of computer from the same manufacturer are incompatible. To make it even more confusing, some popular computers (such as the larger IBM minicomputers) offer a choice of several commonly used operating systems.

In Chapter 7, we shall discuss the range of packages available on the market. However, our main concern in this book is with *systems analysis*: to analyse the information needs of the business, and to design and implement a system which meets those needs. Even if an application package can be found to meet precisely those needs, this still only represents a small part of the problem.

If you think back to managing the burger bar, it is not just a question of getting a microcomputer and some accounting software. You need first to think about getting software that does exactly what you want; you then need to learn how to use it, and after that, you have to enter lots of data in. Remember that about 25% of small businesses that buy microcomputers don't get around to using them properly. Using computers is not very difficult, but it does require effort.

Questions

7 List the types of computer software which are likely to be most appropriate for business applications.
8 If computer programs had to be specially written for such applications, what expertise would be required from the staff responsible for designing and writing these programs?

For question 7, we could give quite a long list of software, and we shall obviously discuss various applications in more detail later in this book. Chapter 1 has already given a fairly strong clue as to which applications are important. The most obvious applications, common to most businesses, are:

- Sales ledger/invoicing
- Purchase ledger/payment of suppliers
- Nominal ledger/internal accounting
- Stock control
- Payroll
- Word processing/mailing.

Regarding question 8, writing computer programs is extremely expensive, and even large companies often avoid producing their own programs if they can; indeed, nobody would consider writing their own word processing software, because this is a very standard application, for which excellent software is available relatively cheaply. However, it is sometimes necessary to develop software from scratch, and the next section discusses the type of staff required to do this.

Expertise needed to produce software

Large businesses often still commission their own software, especially for accounting applications, for reasons which will be discussed shortly. To produce software, requires two specific kinds of expertise:

1 To understand the requirements of business managers, and to specify computer software which meets those requirements, and to ensure that the programs meet the specifications when they are eventually fully written and tested.

2 To fully understand the capabilities of the computer hardware, and to be totally conversant in the computer language which is to be used to write the programs, and to be expert in the arts of programming.

The first role requires someone with a broad understanding of business, and is the role of the *systems analyst*. The second role requires a skilled technician, a *computer programmer*. The two roles are clearly complementary, and both are necessary. Sometimes the two roles are combined by an *analyst programmer*, especially where a fourth generation language is used which requires relatively little programming effort.

Developing software for major applications is extremely expensive. Consultancy companies charge currently about £300–£400 per day for experienced programmers and £500–£600 per day for analysts, and a large project may take several man years to complete. New software developments costing several hundred thousand pounds (or even several million pounds) have therefore become common.

Software written for a specific application is often refered to as *bespoke software*, just as bespoke clothing is specifically made to measure for one particular person. We now consider some alternative and more economical approaches to buying software.

Packages and tailored software

For many applications, particularly for small businesses, the cost of commissioning bespoke software is likely to be prohibitive. One alternative, obvious to any of you who are familiar with home computers, is to buy a *computer package*: a piece of 'off the shelf' software designed to process the particular application. For example, there are probably over one hundred microcomputer packages on the UK market designed to handle sales ledger and invoicing. Some of these are better than others, and they vary in the flexibility they offer.

The better, and more expensive, microcomputer packages allow users to design reports to their own specifications. They may also allow some flexibility in how accounts are set up; however, a package is unlikely to do *exactly* what is required.

Packages have a number of advantages over bespoke software:

● They are much cheaper, because the development costs can be spread over many users, whereas the cost of bespoke software is borne by only one user
● They are often more 'user-friendly' than bespoke software, because they have been developed over a long period of time, allowing the design of the software to be influenced by the views of users. Software companies also tend to be aware of competing products, and ready to adopt any good ideas that their competitors develop

● New versions are produced periodically, to take advantage of developments in hardware and software, and to incorporate any changes in government policy and legislation.

The last point is an extremely important one. We often see large companies with apparently very 'old-fashioned' systems running on modern computers, when they are using software written for them several years before, which has not been upgraded. Why not? Because it takes too much effort and is too costly. Often, companies using such software do not realize how poor it is, because they have not seen anything better. Poor software costs money, because it is more difficult to use and therefore entering data takes longer; staff will also make more mistakes, and spend more time correcting them.

Financial software almost certainly has to be upgraded when changes in government policy occur. This applies particularly to tax changes in the case of accounting software, while payroll software requires very frequent updating as the rules for National Insurance and pensions may also be changed. The advantage of a package is that such updates are provided at a fairly low cost by the software company (usually referred to as a *software house*).

Question

9 Given the advantages of packaged software, why do businesses pay to have programs written?

The first reason is that programs are sometimes written for relatively small tasks, such as carrying out some simple calculations to analyse market research data. Such 'one-off' jobs can sometimes be programmed very easily, and it may not be worth buying a package, even if one is available.

The second reason is that businesses often use database software, which incorporates a fourth generation language. This can vastly reduce the amount of programming time involved and hence reduces the development costs. This means that businesses can afford to have their own programs written, where no suitable package is available.

However, the major reason is that businesses often find that none of the packages available does everything that they want. Businesses develop systems of their own for coping with their particular accounting problems. Generally, a package will only go 80% or 90% of the way towards doing what they need. The question then is: is it worth changing their system in order to be able to use a package? Often the answer is no, because the cost of changing an accounting system may be high, because of the need to use new stationery and to retrain staff. Using a package may also mean losing some flexibility in dealing with exceptional situations, and this may be unacceptable.

Another alternative, often used, is to adapt a standard package to cope with your own requirements. The programming work is usually carried out by the software house, who will charge extra for any modifications to the standard package. This is referred to as *tailored software*, because the software has been 'tailored' to your particular specifications. Tailored software is obviously more expensive than buying a standard package, but is very much cheaper than writing a suite of programs from scratch.

In many situations, tailored software does provide a very effective solution, but care is needed when the package is upgraded. It is very possible that a specially tailored version of the package will no longer work correctly when the basic package is upgraded. Indeed, some software houses insist on a policy of 'no specials' (i.e. no tailoring) precisely because of this problem.

Questions

Under Plc manufacture warm winter underwear at their factory in the North of England. They employ 1000 manufacturing staff and 500 office staff. They sell the underwear to the public by direct mail order, and also to trade wholesalers on credit; each year, they receive about 120,000 direct mail orders and 3,000 trade orders. They wish to use a computer to issue invoices and process sales accounts.

10 Would you advise Under Plc to use packaged software, tailored software or bespoke software for their sales accounting system? Why?
11 What hardware would Under Plc need to support this system?

Which should be chosen first – hardware or software?

Regarding question 10, the reasons have already been indicated, why a business might make one of these three choices in getting software. A small business would probably not be able to afford anything other than a package, perhaps with slight tailoring. Under Plc are apparently big enough to be able to afford to commission bespoke software if they needed to, but that may well not be necessary. On the other hand, Under Plc are likely to require a number of facilities which are not available in most packages.

For example, Under Plc may want to allow mail order customers the option of paying in instalments, while charging them interest on late payments; many accounting packages do not have this facility. Again, it is likely that Under Plc would want to keep stock quantities for several different sizes on one stock record; many stock control packages only allow for one size per record. Thus, whereas Under Plc might buy an accounting package, one would expect a substantial amount of tailoring to fit their particular requirements.

The two questions are also related, because Under Plc are likely to require more powerful facilities than can be offered by standard microcomputers. If they decide to buy a multi-user computer with the appropriate operating system, then this immediately limits the choice of accounting packages available. Often, there may be only two or three packages offered on a particular computer, and it would not therefore be surprising if none of these met the specifications for Under Plc. It is therefore usually best first to find the most suitable software, and then choose hardware which runs that software.

Regarding question 11, Under Plc process an average of about 500 orders per day. This is probably subject to seasonal variation, so the maximum may be as high as 1000 orders in a day, or perhaps 2500 transactions, allowing for creating invoices and then entering payments. If each transaction took a minute, then one operator could enter 480 transactions in an eight-hour day, and thus at least six operators and hence six VDUs would be required. Other VDUs will be needed to allow managers and accounting staff to access information from the system, and to request the printing of reports. Given that other applications are also likely to be run on the computer, we would expect Under Plc to have a minicomputer with at least 20 to 30 VDUs, and possibly more. A detailed systems study would be necessary in order to be more precise about requirements.

The need for large computers

We have already mentioned briefly the differences between microcomputers, minicomputers and mainframes. If you have used a microcomputer in your college, and also used a larger computer, you will probably have been struck by the advantages of using a microcomputer. These are some of the reasons why microcomputers are preferred by many commercial users, as well as college students:

● Microcomputer software usually has a much better user interface, and is more friendly to use
● You get immediate response from a micro, whereas with a larger computer you have to compete with other users, and may have to wait for ages
● You have total control with a micro, and you don't need to send your output to a distant printer, from which it emerges hours or days later.

There has been a tremendous move away from large computer systems and towards microcomputers in the 1980s. Many users have discovered that they can write their own programs using packages such as Lotus 1-2-3, instead of waiting months for the computer department to write a program for them on the mainframe.

Question

12 Why do many organizations still use mainframe computers?

As you may have realized, the reason was indicated in the example of Under Plc: large information systems need large computers to support them. A large accounting system requires very frequent access by numerous users to a large central database, and networks of microcomputers simply will not cope with such demands. It's like using a small car to tow a ten-ton trailer up a hill; the whole thing will just seize up and refuse to operate.

Another problem with large accounting systems is that they generate enormous amounts of necessary paper; thousands of invoices, and hundreds of pages of reports need to be printed out weekly, or even daily. This requires fast printers, and only relatively powerful computers can support such printers.

Communications links

It is now usually easy to connect computers together, and this provides great flexibility. The physical link may be either a direct cable or a telephone line. For a microcomputer to communicate with another computer, it just requires a suitable communications board to be installed, together with an associated piece of software to control operations. The communications (or comms) board is a printed circuit board containing various chips and other necessary hardware components, which can be installed in a few minutes by a competent computer dealer. Different types of comms boards are needed for different tasks: for example, one board may connect your micro to a telephone link, while another will connect it to an IBM mainframe.

The simplest form of communications link is probably that used by home computer hobbyists, who send messages from one micro to another over a telephone link. Similarly, consultants often bring portable computers to their clients' offices, which they use to enter data. Once the data has been captured, it can be sent over a telephone line to the minicomputer in the consultants' main office, where it is analysed.

Some companies even employ staff to stay at home! The staff concerned are usually employed as programmers or on data entry. They create programs or enter data into files at home, and when these are ready, they simply send them over the telephone line to the main company computer. This saves the staff the time and cost of going to work, and it saves the company all the overheads of providing office space for that member of staff. Thus, home working may well be the pattern of the future.

Figures 2.5 and 2.6 show more sophisticated uses of communications links: a *local area network (LAN)* and a mainframe computer with micros used as terminals to the computer.

Local area networks (LAN), as in Figure 2.5, are becoming increasingly common. The advantage of such a system is that each user can use his microcomputer independently for most of the time, but has the option of sharing files and software with other users via the central file server. Sometimes, a microcomputer with a hard

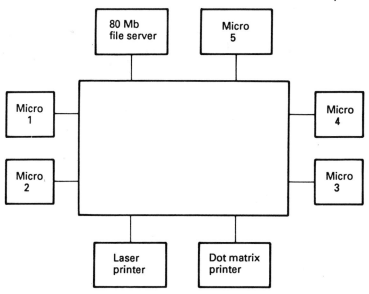

Each microcomputer can operate independently, or can connect to the network to access the file server and printers, and communicate with the other microcomputers.

Figure 2.5 A local area network

disk is used instead of a dedicated file server. Another advantage of a network is that you can share facilities with other users, which reduces the cost per user for more expensive printers such as lasers. In addition to the file server, a LAN requires a set of special cables and connectors; the best-known systems are probably Ethernet and the IBM Token Ring system. It also requires suitable network software; a number of companies produce these for IBM-compatible micros, including Novell, 3COM, and Torus.

The use of microcomputers as terminals to mainframe computers, as shown in Figure 2.6, is now standard in many large businesses. This approach enables users to get the best of both worlds. On the one hand, you can access the central company databases or the sophisticated software packages available on the mainframe. On the other hand, you can use the microcomputer on its own, when you find this more convenient; you may even decide to extract some of the

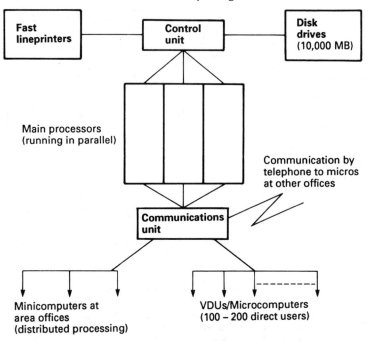

Figure 2.6   A typical mainframe configuration

data from the central database, and analyse it on your microcomputer spreadsheet package.

Question

13 Your college has decided that each student must be given a printed transcript of all of his/her exam and coursework grades. The current student records are kept on a microcomputer in the faculty office; each tutor is to be given access to a microcomputer to enter the grades for their subject. The eventual grades are to be printed on the lineprinter attached to the main college computer. What hardware and software will be needed for this system?

This proposal presents certain practical difficulties because some of your tutors might refuse to use computers, and the college authorities might consider the system excessively expensive for what it does. Nevertheless, it is certainly a feasible proposal, at least in principle.

In hardware terms, the solution is straightforward: all that is required is a microcomputer and file server in the faculty office, linked by a network to microcomputers in the various staff offices. The basic student records can be entered by the faculty office: comprising student number, name, home address, course code, date of birth, and so on. Individual tutors can then request from the system the names of students on a particular course and year, and enter the grades against them, using the microcomputer in their own staff office. When complete, the lists of grades can be printed off and checked in the faculty office. For the final stage, a link from the network to the main college computer is desirable. The names and grades can be sent to the main college computer, where they can be printed and automatically cut and folded into individual student letters, thus saving considerable clerical effort.

All that is required is the software to do this! If the programs had to be written from scratch, it would cost a significant amount of time and money. Fortunately, certain UK colleges and universities have already developed their own software for precisely this purpose.

The major problem we see is of systems feasibility. First, there is the cost: is such an expenditure (probably upwards of £20,000) really justified? Secondly, we would be extremely concerned about confidentiality and accuracy of the data on this system. What is to prevent a student accessing the system, and changing their grades, or finding out the grades for other students? This raises serious issues, which we will come back to later in this book.

Computing needs of a large business

We have discussed in outline what computers can do for business; both large and small businesses now make enormous use of computers. However, the approach is often very different, and we shall discuss why, in the remainder of this chapter.

Large businesses have traditionally been dominated by computer departments running large and rather inflexible systems on mainframe computers. As has already been mentioned, there are good reasons why they need to continue running large centralized information systems. On the other hand, microcomputers are now very much part of the scene, and many staff regularly use microcomputers, who would not have touched a computer in the past. Microcomputers are usually paid for by departments, rather than from a central budget, but most large companies have policies about what makes of hardware and which computer packages may be bought, in order to achieve some reasonable degree of standardization.

The hardware configuration shown in Figure 2.6 is reasonably typical of what one might expect to see in a large business. There are certain key applications that would need to be run on a large central computer, such as accounting, payroll and so on. Such applications will involve the use of large databases, shared by many users, with a high number of transactions to the input. The central computer may also be used as the hub of an electronic mailing system, to send internal messages around the company.

Apart from the major applications, large businesses tend to have a very wide range of small applications, mostly ideally suited to running on a microcomputer. Areas such as marketing analysis, financial planning, and forecasting of manpower needs, often require a certain amount of computer analysis, and there is now a wide range of microcomputer packages on the market to meet all types of specialist needs. If a suitable package is not available, it may not be a major operation to write a computer program to do the job, because the task involved is often relatively simple. This contrasts with accounting, which has already been mentioned; that would require a large suite of programs, making it expensive to write your own software.

Organization structure of a large computer department

Figure 2.7 shows a typical organization structure for the computer department in a large business. Most large businesses have such computer departments, although sometimes the department has a title such as *Data Processing* (DP) or *Management Information Systems*. In the example shown here, there are broadly five categories of staff:

1 *Systems analysts* who analyse and design systems, and specify computer solutions to meet user requirements, and oversee implementation of the new systems.
2 *Programmers* who write programs, where necessary. Often, their

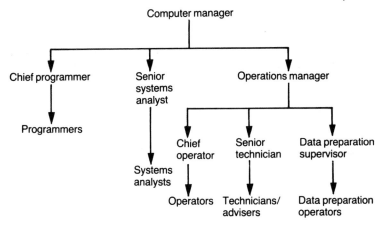

Figure 2.7 Organizational structure of a large computer department

main functions are to update existing programs and to help with the implementation of complex packages.

3 *Operators* whose main function is to operate the central computer. This includes loading new software and data files, unloading printouts, and scheduling and placing tasks in priority in the computer at busy times.

4 *Technicians* who provide an extremely important support to users around the organization, especially in relation to microcomputers. This can include connecting up a new printer, finding out why a microcomputer is not working, or helping out new users who do not know what they are doing.

5 *Data preparation staff.* Their job is to enter data into the central computer, normally for applications such as accounting which have a large number of daily transactions, and are therefore best processed in batches.

Other companies will have computer departments which are structured slightly differently from this. For example, it is becoming common to combine the roles of programmer and analyst. However, the needs of the organization are likely to be very much along the lines indicated.

Many other posts are found in large computer departments other than those mentioned; some common examples are network managers, database administrators and media librarians, but there are others.

Question

14 Chateau Bottlers Ltd are a small wine importer, which buy selected French wines and sell them to hotels and restaurants. They employ twelve office staff, together with the managing director. CB Ltd only deal with administration and planning; the actual work of transporting, bottling and warehousing wine is undertaken by subcontractors for them. What would you expect their computing requirements to be?

Computing needs of a small business

The example in this question is very typical of many small businesses who successfully use microcomputers. It is quite likely that a single microcomputer will be enough to meet Chateau Bottlers' needs. If not, a network of three or four microcomputers will certainly suffice.

The most relevant applications are likely to be stock control, invoicing and sales accounting (particularly as many of their clients are likely to buy on credit from CB Ltd). They might also wish to use the computer for regular mailings of their clients, in order to promote any specially good wines that they are selling. It is also possible that they might wish to use the microcomputer for other applications, including word processing, payroll and financial planning.

What CB Ltd will not have is a large computer department with a wide range of expertise. Indeed, they are quite likely to have no knowledge whatsoever of computers. The most important point for them is to make sure that they can find good advice before they proceed, both from other similar businesses and from a good, reputable dealer.

Assignment 2

Select a local, small business and for that business:
(a) List the information-related tasks in that business for which a computer could be used.

(b) Find details of a microcomputer package suitable for each of these tasks (the best source is one of the microcomputer magazines aimed at business users).

(c) Explain the advantages of using a microcomputer in each case

Recap

Effective *information systems* are essential to a business, to provide the information that is required to run the business and also to establish good financial control.

The major reason for using computers in business is to support information systems. As well as reducing costs, computers can also provide much better information.

Microcomputers are very widely used by businesses, but larger businesses need *minicomputers* or *mainframes* to allow many users simultaneous access to large databases. Small businesses generally use microcomputers.

Packages can be purchased for most major applications, and are normally the most cost-effective solution (for small businesses, the only solution). *Tailored software* often provides a better solution than a package, but at a slightly higher cost. *Bespoke software* is likely to be prohibitively expensive for major applications, but is sometimes a necessary choice for large businesses.

Computer (or data processing) departments can include a wide range of skills: systems analysts, programmers, operators, technicians and data preparation staff. Small businesses usually lack such expertise.

Answers

1 Name, address, contact name, telephone no., invoice no., date of invoice, amount, date paid, current balance.

2 See Figure 2.4

3 It could save on clerical costs, and provide better management control and better management information.

4 Processor to control operations and perform calculations. Memory to provide immediate temporary storage. Screen/keyboard to interrogate the computer, and type in data. Printer to produce 'hard copy' – printed output.
Disk to provide permanent storage.

5 50 × 152 bytes per supplier = 7600 bytes. Perhaps 11 or 12KB would be needed to allow for overheads.

6 Enter new supplier details,
Enter new supplier address,
Enter amount for new invoice,
Enter total amount paid,
Run end-of-month routine.

7 Sales ledger/invoicing; purchase ledger/payment of suppliers; nominal ledger/internal accounting; stock control; payroll; word processing/mailing

8 To understand the requirements of business managers, and to ensure that the software meets their needs (systems analyst). To understand the capabilities of the hardware, and to be expert at writing computer programs (programmer).

9 For small 'one-off' tasks.
Where they use a 4GL, so that programming is relatively easy.
Because no package does what they need.

10 Preferably, buy packaged software. Bespoke software may be the best option if Under Plc are large enough to afford it, and if no package meets their needs.

11 Probably at least a minicomputer with 20 to 30 VDUs.

12 Most large companies have mainframe computers; almost all have large minicomputers if they do not have mainframes.

13 Microcomputer network with link to main college computer. Suitable educational administration package.

14 Microcomputer, or possibly a small network. Software for accounting, invoicing, stock control.

3: Initiating the systems development life cycle

Objectives

After reading this chapter, you will be able to:

- Explain what is meant by the term *system* within the context of business
- Describe the features of a system which may give rise to a 'problem'
- State who are the users, direct and indirect, of a system, and roles played by these users in identifying systems problems
- Describe the cyclical nature of systems development
- Outline the importance of a carefully prepared start to the systems development life cycle through a well-considered feasibility study.

Scenario

You work as an orders clerk for a wine and spirit wholesaler, Ongar Winemart. The company has a large warehouse which stocks beer, wine and spirits. These are bought either directly from the manufacturers or, for foreign-produced alcohol, from import agents. From this warehouse, cases of bottles of alcohol are supplied to a large number of retail outlets, some of which are specialist wine merchants and others, including small grocery 'corner shops'.

Ongar Winemart operates two basic methods of dealing with customers' purchases. The first and simplest arrangement is that the customer arrives at the warehouse and buys, for cash, from the available stock. This is sometimes known as a *cash and carry* operation.

The alternative method is for the customer to place the order by telephone with an order clerk, who tells the customer whether the required goods are available. The order is delivered on a particular day in the week, depending upon the delivery van's route schedule. It is possible that the customer will make two or even three telephone orders in a week. These would be amalgamated to form a single delivery.

This scenario shows but a small part of the total business operation, namely orders from customers. It tells us nothing about Ongar Winemart's procedures in ordering from its suppliers, nor about how it keeps a check on stock levels and availability. But, as we shall see, in identifying a 'problem' on the selling side of the business, we can often make just a passing reference to other facets of the business operation.

Questions

1 What is meant by a 'system'?
2 What is a systems 'problem' and how does it arise?

The concept of systems

A *system* can be described as a set of ingredients or elements which interact and communicate with one another to achieve some purpose. Our own bodies, for example, constitute highly complex systems designed to enable us to survive. Messages are being sent continuously between the various parts such as the brain, nerve endings, muscles, and so on.

Business, too, is a system made up of a number of constituent parts, or sub-systems. These sub-systems need to communicate with one another in order to achieve their common objective. So, in the case of our wholesaler, Ongar Winemart, the common objectives are to meet the customers' requirements and thereby earn sufficient money to pay staff wages and other costs of staying in business.

The overall system might, for ease of operating, be divided into a number of sub-systems as follows:

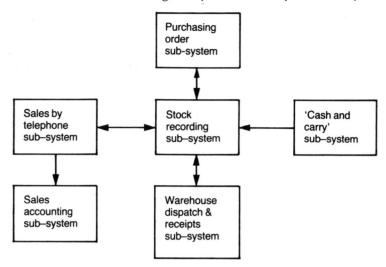

Figure 3.1   A business system is divided into sub-systems

There will be other sub-systems in the overall system, as explained in Chapter 1, including procedures to deal with staff and payment of wages. But for our purposes, it is quite sufficient to consider only those sub-systems shown in Figure 3.1. We should also note the linkages, which reveal the need for information to be communicated from one sub-system to another.

Let us consider the two types of customers, starting with the 'cash and carry' buyer. He arrives at the warehouse in the expectation that the goods he wants are in stock, walks around pushing a trolley into which he places his purchases. If the particular brand of spirits he wants is not available, he will look at alternatives which are available and decide which is the most suitable substitute or replacement item. When the customer has assembled everything he wants, he pays for the goods at the check-out desk.

Suppose you want to 'promote' a particular product as a 'special offer'. You will arrange to place cases of the product in a prominent position, adjacent to large advertising notices. The customer, you hope, will notice the special promotion and be persuaded to buy the product concerned.

Thus, the 'cash and carry' customer presents few difficulties; he decides when to arrive, what to buy, and pays immediately; and company staff do not have to get involved in active selling to the customer. In terms of adjacent sub–systems, the customer's purchases will affect the amount of cash taken, little more than simple entries in a ledger, and stock recording.

Now let us consider the other type of customer, the one who orders goods by telephone. He may telephone you at any time during normal working-hours. The greater the number of such customers, the greater the quantity of resources, human and machine, that must be available in order to ensure that the customer is not kept waiting an unacceptably long time for a response.

Suppose you are the orders clerk on duty when the customer has got through to the office. The first thing you will need to do is establish the customer's identity. How are you to do this in the absence of a visual document?

Question

3 List the reasons why the order clerk at Ongar Winemart should be able to identify a customer who makes an order by telephone.

It may be that you can recognize the customer's voice, but this is not a totally reliable method. Perhaps all regular customers have their own unique identity code number which the customer quotes to you. That would enable you to recognize an existing customer. But how, then, do you recognize a genuine potential *new* customer? So, even at this point of initial contact we see that there is scope for potential problems.

Once the issue of customer identification has been sorted out, we get to the second stage. This is where the customer says that he wants certain goods. Suppose the customer asks for ten cases of Glenglen whisky. How do you, sitting at a desk in an office, know how many cases are in stock in the warehouse? Perhaps a computer system is in use. In this case you may be able to look up the records stored on the computer files.

If you sell goods to a customer, you will also have to be able to inform the computer system in order to prevent their being sold a second time to somebody else.

And what do you do if the stock recording sub-system is not computerized? The answer would seem to be that you will have to check the stock availability in person. You would also take some action to ensure that the same stock is not later sold to somebody else.

Dealing with telephone orders manually in this way is slow and tedious; if the desired goods are not available it will be necessary to tell the customer and suggest possible substitute items.

It seems quite clear that dealing with orders over the telephone is more easily accommodated if a good computer system is in operation. But this is not quite sufficient. After all, the computer record may not be accurate. 'Shrinkage' through theft or breakages may leave the actual stock at a lower level than the computer system would indicate.

That brings us to yet another problem – how to handle shortages. Suppose the customer had ordered ten cases of Glenglen whisky but there are only six in stock. Had the customer been at the warehouse he could have chosen an alternative very quickly, but over the telephone there is a need to indicate what else is available to make up the shortfall, and your idea of a suitable substitute may not be the same as his.

Furthermore, there is the little matter of special promotions. The 'cash and carry' customer sees the displays; but the telephone customer would need to be told about them. But would you always remember to tell the customers?

It is possible, as we will see in later chapters, to develop computer systems which help overcome many of the problems we have identified here. But we must also consider that other equipment, such as telephones and telephone lines, will be required; and, above all, the system must be designed for human use and cater for human wants and needs.

Systems 'problems'

In the text above we have referred to certain 'difficulties' or 'problems'. These could be described as *operational problems*, that is, complications in carrying out the planned course of action. This is different from a *systems problem* which would imply that there is something about the very system or plan which is inherently weak. So how might we identify a systems problem as against an operational problem?

In practice it may be difficult to distinguish clearly one type of problem from the other. Our starting-point could be to look for clearly stated *objectives* or targets. All systems require objectives which can be measured so as to enable us to see whether the target is met.

For example, Ongar Winemart might have as an objective that a customer's order over the telephone line should be completed within two minutes. If all goes according to plan, as an orders clerk you should be able to handle thirty orders each hour. It would be a simple matter to count the actual number of orders you handle and see whether it averages at thirty or more per hour.

Questions

4 Suppose Ongar Winemart expects you to process at least thirty telephone orders each working hour and your actual average is only 25, does this signify a systems problem or an operation problem?
5 List all the possible causes of your failure to meet the set target.

Let us treat both questions together. Suppose the target is not met. This may be the result of an unexpected operational situation such as:

1   Fewer telephone orders than expected.
2   The telephone lines being temporarily out of order.
3   A larger than expected number of new customers opening accounts.

A systems problem is likely to manifest itself in a similar way, but the root causes are different. For example, it is all very well having a quantifiable objective, but the objective must be capable of being met by current resources and in the light of demands being placed on the system. If the computer system slows down and produces a long response time when there are four or more simultaneous users, then using such a system with six or more order clerks using the computer at the same time is bound to cause difficulties; such problems would be inherent in the system.

In attempting to identify a systems problem, there is a need for us to consider the possible sources of difficulty. These might include:

1   Deficiencies in the performance of current equipment; poor response time is a symptom.
2   Shortcomings in procedures relating to the part of the system under consideration. For example, inadequate clerical procedures in dealing with multiple telephone orders may lead to errors in instructions to the delivery van drivers.

3   Weaknesses in adjacent procedures. As an example of this, it may
    be that the telephone order handling procedures are adequate, but
    there may be failures in the warehouse stock recording system
    which cannot easily be detected by the orders clerk.

Users of the system

A system may display serious weaknesses for months or even years
before any urgent attempt is made to overcome them. The key factor
in initiating changes by starting the systems development life cycle, is
the stance taken by the *users* of the system. The users can be divided
into three main categories:

1   *Direct users.* These are the regular day-to-day users of the current
    system. They directly suffer from the frustrations of the system
    not performing as well as it ought. Very often, direct users are
    worried that their job performances may be judged without regard
    for the poor back-up procedures and facilities. For example, your
    manager might suggest that you are not working hard enough
    using as evidence the number of orders you take; but he may not
    take sufficient account of poor computer response time and
    inadequate back-up information.

2   *Indirect users* do not normally operate the system in a direct
    manner, but benefit from reports and other information generated
    by the system. Such indirect users at Ongar Winemart would
    probably include the managers of the Telephone Order
    department and the warehouse, both of whom receive summary
    reports on orders taken.

3   *Administrative users* have even less formal contact with the system,
    but are in close touch with its consequences. These users are
    normally senior members of staff and extremely influential.
    Within the context of our telephone ordering system, the relevant
    administrative users might include:

    ● The company accountant, who is concerned about the flows of
      stocks and money and is therefore interested in having a system
      which enables as much money as possible, to be earned quickly
      without being tied up in unsold stock
    ● The sales director, who will want to ensure that as great a
      quantity of goods as possible is sold.

If we relate these categories of users to the personnel hierarchy as mentioned in Chapter 1, the most senior personnel are likely to be the administrative users; at the next level down, the managers are the indirect users; at the base of the hierarchy are the operatives, the direct users.

Any of the three groups of users may try to get changes introduced, but if the systems development life cycle is to get under way, the initiative will normally come from the indirect users. However, for a proposed new system to be fully developed and put into operation, the active support of the administrative users is vital.

The systems development life cycle

Suppose you and a group of friends decided to spend a week walking in the Brecon Beacons, but none of you had any experience of walking and camping, nor did you have the necessary equipment. Would you simply walk into a camping equipment shop on the first day of your holiday, buy some gear, and then make your way to the railway station to start your journey?

We would imagine that you would not be so foolish as to undertake a hazardous holiday without some preparation. So how do you plan your holiday?

What you would do is engage in a cycle of activity. First, deciding what type of holiday; secondly, deciding where to go; thirdly, listing the equipment that will be required; fourthly, calculating the costs. Let us stop there for a moment and think about what you would be doing.

Each stage leads to the next. For example, deciding where to go will depend to some extent on the type of holiday you want. But it could be the case that the result of a later stage of planning may lead you to re-think an earlier stage. For example, as a result of calculating the costs involved, you may have to rethink where to go or even what type of holiday to take.

Let us say that these initial plans are complete and you know what you are going to do, where you are going to go, what equipment you need and how much it will cost. But remember, you have had no experience of this type of holiday; indeed, you have never even erected a tent. It would therefore be prudent to test the equipment and your ability to use it before embarking on your holiday. You may discover some fault or inadequacy that needs to be rectified. Or you may even discover that you cannot carry the sheer weight of the camping and other gear for long periods of time, and this could lead you to rethink your entire holiday plans, in other words you go back to the first stage in the planning process. This is an example of a development life cycle.

Business systems also require planning and other preparatory procedures; these, too, involve a development life cycle, a set of activities which are carried out to develop and implement a business information system.

Many experts refer to six stages in the systems development life cycle as shown in Figure 3.2. These are:

1 The *preliminary investigation*. This is the first stage and we will be examining the activities involved in some detail later in this chapter. For the moment we can say that in this stage we consider whether it is worth investigating and changing the current system.

2 The *detailed investigation* into what the various users want and need from the system. The various techniques which we may use are considered in detail in the next chapter.

3 The *design of the system*. This is where the systems analyst designs the *logical system*, that is:

● The outputs that are required from the system such as report and screen layouts
● The inputs to the system including the input media and format
● The processing 'rules' and conditions including methods of security
● The linkages and communication between one part of the system and another
● The human procedures such as how clerical staff access computer data and what they should do to get the computer to produce required reports. '

Increasingly these days, *prototyping* is used as an aid to design. A prototyping system allows for rapid amendment to output and input formats and processing rules and is commonly associated with *fourth generation development tools*. We will be discussing prototyping in Chapter 8.

4 The *development of software*. This, for larger companies, often means the writing of computer programs to perform specified

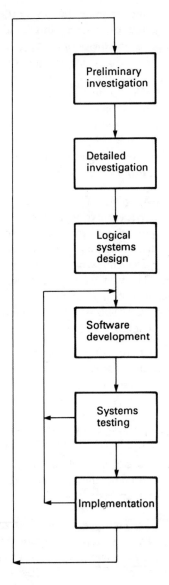

Figure 3.2   System development life cycle

functions and operations. For smaller organizations, employment of specialist computer programmers is often too costly and so they are more likely to buy off-the-shelf *applications packages*. But no matter what the source of the programs, they must be installed on the organization's computer system ready for the next stage, systems testing.

5   *Systems testing*. The purpose is to ensure that:
  ● The individual programs do what they are intended to do, that is that they follow the rules and conditions as laid down
  ● The overall system performs according to the specification
  ● The various component parts of the system link together properly
  ● The systems behave in the way expected.

6   *Implementation*, where the system has completed its tests and trials and is installed ready for use by the users.

The role of systems analysis and design
The six stages in the development life cycle are activities in which a person known as a *systems analyst* is intimately involved, and activities are collectively known as *systems analysis and design*.
Systems analysis is the process of:

1   Gathering and interpreting facts.
2   Diagnosing problems.
3   Using the facts to improve the system.

Certainly the first two stages in the systems development life cycle come under this heading. It is also suggested that a large part of the third stage, especially when prototyping is used, will also come under this heading.

   It would be as well, at this point, to offer words of caution and to talk about what systems analysis is *not*:

1   It is *not* about deciding which procedures should be converted from manual to computer-based methods. This decision, if it is made, should be as a *result of the findings of the study* and not pre-determined.
2   It is *not* about deciding what changes to make to procedures. It is a study of current procedures. As in 1 above, any changes should be as a result of the study.

3   It is *not* about finding the best technical solution. Modern business systems involve a mixture of human and technical facilities working together. What might appear to be an excellent technical solution may prove unworkable if not acceptable to human operatives.

Systems design is the design of a new system or improvements to the old. The design stage includes the testing and implementation stages of the systems development life cycle.

Question

6 List the personal qualities you might expect a competent systems analyst to possess.

Look at your answer to question 6. Did you include the ability to program the computer? It is commonly believed that the systems analyst is some kind of computer programmer. In fact, many systems analysts are not, and never have been programmers. The detailed *technical skill* required by the computer programmer is different from the sound knowledge of *business procedures* required by the analyst.

As a fact gatherer, the systems analyst has to be something of a detective; in analysing the facts, he must be able to distingish facts from opinions and relevant information from 'red herrings'. As a designer, he must be able to distinguish user 'needs' from 'wants' and know what equipment and trained people are able to do and not necessarily be able to do it himself.

Starting the systems development process

Staying with our example of Ongar Winemart, suppose the company decides to investigate the telephone ordering system. There could be a number of reasons for this decision. These might include:

1   Customers might have complained that they could not get through easily on the telephone because the system always seemed to be engaged.
2   Customers might have grumbled that even when they did get

through, the order-handling system proved tedious and negotiations protracted because the clerks were uncertain of stock availability.

3   The order department manager might have calculated that the orders clerks generally handled fewer orders per hour than expected.

4   The sales director might have complained that sales of goods on 'special offer' were less successful than expected, suggesting that the order clerks were not trying hard enough to persuade customers to place orders for them.

There are just four reasons that indicate that something is wrong with the system. Of course, we cannot immediately tell whether there is something inherently wrong with the system, or whether the system is just being poorly operated. This is something that the company's management hope the systems analyst will be able to tell them.

The preliminary investigation

This, as was stated earlier, is the first stage in the systems development life cycle. Somebody in the organization, perhaps the departmental manager or perhaps the sales director or chief accountant, initiates a request for assistance with a systems problem, this assistance hopefully culminating in a new or revised system being introduced into the organization. This preliminary investigation, in turn, is in four phases:

1   *Proposal definition.* This is normally a short document explaining the needs for a feasibility study and the scope of the study. The contents will normally include:
   ● A list of the persons proposing the project and having an interest in the outcome of the study
   ● The business reason for the study; this might include a brief comment on the apparent deficiencies of the system as currently run
   ● A comment on the organizational support for the study
   ● Schedule considerations such as timing of the study and the need for access to user management and staff.

2   *Request clarification.* Even a short document with contents as shown above, might not be totally clear. It is therefore necessary

for the analyst to examine the document to ensure that the terms of reference are unambiguous. If there are any doubts, it is essential that the analyst finds out precisely what is wanted.

3 *The feasibility study.* This is an initial study to consider whether it is worth going ahead with a full-blown systems analysis and design exercise. Of course, in making the request for assistance with a systems problem, the initiating manager hopes that it is feasible to do so, but he must consider that possibility that this will not be the case. There are a number of facets of feasibility that will need to be investigated:

● *Technical feasibility.* The major question here is whether the proposed system can be implemented given the existing equipment. This, in turn, can be sub-divided into further parts. First, can the existing equipment in the possession of the organization cope with the extra demands placed on it by the proposed new system? If the answer is yes, then technical feasibility is met. If the answer is no, then there is a need to ask a second question. Is there equipment available for sale or rent which will meet the organization's systems requirement? If the answer is no, then the system is not feasible. If it is yes, then there is a need to ask a third question about the sophistication of the equipment relative to the organization's technical experience. In other words, it is possible that the equipment that exists is too complicated for the organization and is the proverbial 'sledgehammer to crack a nut'!

● *Economic feasibility.* This can be simply stated as whether the benefits which accrue from the introduction of a new system will outweigh the costs of its introduction. In order to achieve the benefits from the new system it will be necessary to incur expenditure on systems analysis and design, and possibly on new equipment, staff retraining, etc. These costs can be calculated over the expected life of the project. Quite simply, will the additional revenue and/or running cost savings exceed these additional costs? These are sometimes known as *tangible* costs and benefits.

In addition, the feasibility study will need to look at *intangible* costs and benefits, that is those benefits which cannot easily be measured. For example, the new system might be able to provide management with more up-to-date information on sales trends more quickly. This could be beneficial to the organization, though the value of such a benefit is difficult to measure.

- ✓● *Operational feasibility*. The elementary question that will need to be considered is whether the system would work and be used if it were developed and installed. This requires an assessment of the working climate of the department in which the system is introduced. There is a need to consider the attitude of the potential direct users; if they resist the introduction of the new system it may prove to be uneconomic.

- ✓● *Motivational feasibility*. This is an examination of the desire of the organization, and in particular of senior personnel, to introduce the new system. This is particularly important if the direct users are lukewarm in attitude; it will require a positive desire on the part of senior staff to introduce the new system if it is to have any real chance of succeeding.

- ✓● *Schedule feasibility*. This consideration of whether the proposed systems development work can be completed within the time schedule and with the resources allocated to it. You might note, incidentally, that if the feasibility study shows a deficiency of staff for timely completion of the project, employment of additional staff may not necessarily solve the problem because it takes some time to assimilate and induct new members of staff.

4 *Request approval*. This is the final phase of the preliminary investigation, where the request to go ahead with the systems development project is approved. Of course, not all projects are feasible, and these should not be given approval.

All that has happened, so far, is that management has been told that the proposed new or revised system is feasible and warrants a full systems investigation and analysis and thus a move forward to the next stage in the systems development life cycle. This is considered in detail in the next chapter.

Assignment 3

The department of the college at which you are studying has several members of teaching staff with common teaching and research interests. Select a group of staff with such interests and undertake a feasibility study to consider whether it is worth their while developing a common collection (or database) of academic articles and papers which would be stored on a large microcomputer system.

The idea being put forward is that the microcomputer will have a document reader attached to it which will read and convert articles and papers in journals and magazines into a form that could be stored centrally. Individual members of staff would have access to the computerized store of articles and could print off copies at will. The benefits would include the elimination of duplication of pieces of paper stored in each staff room and the immediate and easy availability of the latest information.

Recap

A *system* is a group of elements which interact and communicate with one another.

Business systems can generally be divided into sub-systems, with an *information system* being the means of communication between the constituent parts. All business systems require *objectives* or *targets* if they are to function properly and be adequately controlled. Absence of objectives will often lead to *systems problems*, where the system appears to be out of control.

Business systems can also suffer from *operational problems* as a result of procedures not being followed or through temporary setbacks beyond the organization's control.

The prime mover for change and development of new systems is the stance taken by *users* of the system. Users fall into the following categories:

1 *Direct users*, the operatives who are in direct contact with the system.
2 *Indirect users*, normally the departmental managers who benefit from output reports produced by the system.
3 *Administrative users*, often senior managers and other personnel who have an administrative interest in the system and the effects of its successful or unsuccessful operating.

The development of systems is a cyclical progression in which there are six main stages:

1 The *preliminary investigation*, in which it is decided as a result of a *feasibility study* whether to go ahead with a full systems development.

2 The *detailed investigation* of the existing system gathers facts about how the systems works and how the various parts communicate and interact.

3 The *design of the system* including the outputs, inputs, processing rules and human operations. A modern development is the use of *prototyping* as a means of rapid development of new systems.

4 The *development of software*, which may be written 'in-house' by the organizations own computer programmers. Smaller organizations are more likely to use standard *applications packages*, in which the programs are pre-written and pre-tested.

5 *Systems testing*, which applies to any new system which is installed, including purchased applications packages.

6 *Implementation*, the installation of the new business system, including the human activities. This will therefore include such things as training.

The person responsible for the bulk of the work in the systems development life cycle is the *systems analyst*, who is generally employed for his knowledge of business systems rather than for computing knowledge and skills.

Answers

1 A system is a series of interlocking elements or components designed to achieve some end.

2 A systems problem exists where the system is malfunctioning as a result of some inherent failure. This failure might be automatically detected if there is a properly constructed control mechanism; in other cases it may be manifested as an operational failure without there necessarily appearing to be a fundamental fault.

3 The order clerk should be able to recognize customers for a number of reasons. First, to avoid possible fraud by people merely posing as genuine customers. Failure to detect such fraud not only causes financial loss but also loss of the genuine customers' good will. Secondly, to catch poor payers who still owe the company money and to remind them of their non-payment. It may be company policy not to supply further goods to certain bad payers until payment has been made. Thirdly, to maintain good and friendly relations with customers. Fourthly, to enter correctly the customer's code into the computer system so as to enable the goods ordered and the corresponding financial documents to be sent to the right customer.

4 It could be either.

5 Reasons include:
- Temporary breakdown of telephone equipment
- Inability of computer to respond quickly enough
- Large number of abnormally complex or large orders
- Uneven spread of telephone calls.

6 Qualities include:
- The ability to investigate and gather facts
- Analytical abilities
- An understanding of business systems
- A knowledge and understanding of the aims of information technology
- The ability to specify outputs, inputs, and processing rules that can be followed and acted upon by a specialist computer programmer
- A knowledge of systems development, testing methods and implementation logistics
- An ability to communicate effectively.

4: Determination of system requirements

Objectives

After reading this chapter, you should be able to:

- List the various methods of fact finding available to the systems analyst
- Explain where and how these methods are used, and the advantages and limitations of the various practices
- Outline the techniques which are used to record formally the gathered facts
- Describe the methods used to analyse the data
- Use data flow analysis methods as a means to determine systems requirements
- Explain the advantages of using structured methods of data analysis and, in particular, the use of a 'top down' approach
- Explain how a data dictionary is created and explain its value.

Scenario

Suppose you have left college and have gained employment in the accounts department of Ongar Winemart, the wines and spirits warehouse whose systems problems were featured in Chapter 3. At college you learned about business computing and the Chief Accountant, Mary Anson, has agreed that as part of your training you should be seconded to a team which is to investigate the problems associated with the telephone ordering system.

A feasibility study has already been completed. As a result of this the company has decided to undertake a major systems study. You soon discover that the systems study team is comprised of one person, you.

Organization charts

So here you are, having joined Ongar Winemart just three weeks ago, thrown into the deep end. How do you start?

Your first step is to get to know as much as possible about the organization. In particular you will want to gain a clear knowledge of the formal departmental and hierarchical structures of the organization. But it is also important to remember that an organization contains *people* and that its present position will have been shaped by history.

So a good starting-point is for you to find out something of the history of Ongar Winemart. Many organizations possess literature which contain at least a potted history of themselves, and the Chairman's annual report often contains many details about the company's present position and performance.

In your short time at Ongar Winemart you will no doubt have heard the names of several managers mentioned. But who are they, and what do they do? What are their relative positions, who is senior, and to whom? All this can be quite bewildering until you see or construct an *Organization Chart*. This shows the component departments and units which make up the organization, and the relations between the components.

You may find that part of the organization chart may look something like Figure 4.1.

Note that at this stage we have shown only the main departments and how they are associated with one another.

Now that you know what departments exist in the company, what next? Well, you could try finding out:

1   What the various departments do.

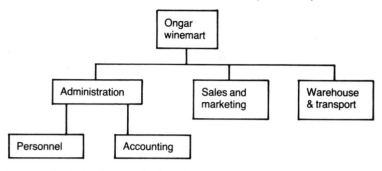

Figure 4.1   A simple organization chart

2   Whether the departments are further sub-divided into sections, and if so what each of those sections does.
3   The names of the people who head or manage each department and section.

This information will prove useful to you when you start to carry out your fact-finding activities. Let us start with the Administration Unit because that is where you are placed. This, as we see, has two departments, one responsible for personnel matters and the other for accounting functions. You may construct an organization chart for the Administration Unit which looks something like Figure 4.2.

Once you have constructed a more detailed organization chart and inserted names, the picture about the formal structure of Ongar Winemart becomes clearer. You can now draw a similar chart for the Sales and Marketing Department, which may look something like Figure 4.3.

Do note that organization charts have limitations:

1   They can get out of date as personnel leave the company and new staff join.
2   Furthermore, the formal structure of the organization may change. For example, payroll may be moved from the personnel department to the accounts department.
3   It shows the *formal* structure and lines of communication. There are also informal structures which never appear on paper. For example, the head buyer, Justin Time, perhaps because of the importance of his job or for social reasons, may have regular contact with and report directly to the Managing Director;

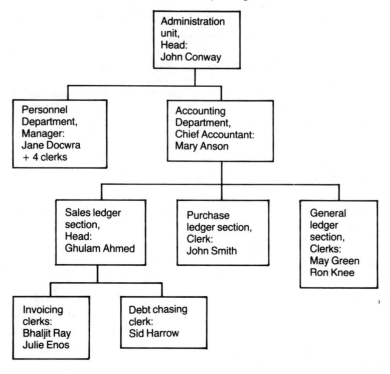

Figure 4.2   An organization chart for the administrative unit

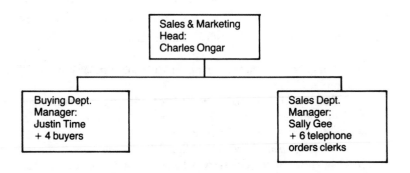

Figure 4.3   An organization chart for the sales and marketing
              department

72

similarly the head of Sales and Marketing might be a favourite nephew of the managing director.

Determination of requirements

You have by now collected a good deal of general information about Ongar Winemart. This should lead you to the people you need to speak to about the systems problems associated with telephone orders. The problem is who to speak first.

Remember, you are trying to find out what the users want from the system and what the currently operated system does.

Questions

2 List the main headings under which you would investigate systems requirements.
3 What are the requirements under each of those main headings?

In answer to questions 2 and 3, it would seem pragmatic to use the following headings:

(a) Basic requirements.
(b) User transactions requirements.
(c) User decision requirements.
(d) Organization-wide requirements.

Let us consider these in turn. First of all, *basic requirements*. Here there are four main elements that you need to consider:

1 The *basic business process*. The kind of questions that you need to ask to elicit the necessary information will include:

- What is this activity intended to achieve?
- What steps are performed?
- Who performs them?
- Where are they performed?
- How long does it take to perform these steps?
- How often are they performed?
- Who uses the resulting information?

2 The *data used and produced during the process*. As a basic requirement you will need to know:
   - What information is needed in order to carry out the basic business process?
   - Where the person carrying out the process gets the information
   - What adjacent processes create or have access to the information?
   - What information is produced as a result of the business process?

3 The *limitations imposed by time considerations and volume of work*. Here you might be expected to seek information about:
   - What triggers the activity?
   - How long the activity takes and whether the task must be completed within a certain period of time?
   - How frequently is the activity undertaken?
   - How many transactions are there which cause this activity to take place and whether the flow of transactions is evenly spread over time?

4 The existence of *performance controls*. Among the issues that you would need to raise are:
   - Whether there are specific performance standards, such as a certain number of transactions per hour or per day
   - How performance standards are checked, and by whom
   - How mistakes in the transaction and errors in the stored data files are dealt with
   - The error rate.

Now let us consider *user transaction requirements*. Here you are concerned with the *direct user*. In a well-structured system you would reasonably expect to find the following attributes:

1 The transactions processing activities are well structured and follow clear-cut routines and a logical sequence.
2 The activities recur frequently, and are highly predictable, and rarely change.
3 The activities have highly structured data requirements.
4 The activities concentrate on current events and are concerned

with the capturing and processing of data with an emphasis on detail.

The questions that you would need to ask would focus on details of the transaction processing. These would include:

- What are the ingredients of the transaction?
- What activates the transaction?
- Who initiates the transaction, how and why?
- How frequently do the transactions occur?
- Are there special circumstances or exceptional conditions that may affect the order?
- What data is needed to process the transaction?
- What information is generated by the transaction and what happens to it?

The third requirement is *user decision requirement*. Decisions are more likely to be taken by managers, or *indirect users*, than by operatives. Decision-making activities have very different characteristics from user transaction activities. In particular:

1 They tend to be structured by the individual or by the requirements of the moment and thus are not part of a routine.
2 They occur irregularly and are thus less predictable.
3 Their data requirements tend to be determined by the individual.
4 They use existing and new data to focus on any time period, perhaps comparing today's results with yesterday's and forecasting tomorrow's.
5 They require a broad outlook, frequently using summary data, rather than narrow detail.

As a systems analyst you would therefore need to ask the relevant managers questions concerning:

- How often and when is information required for decision-making purposes?
- What information is required and where does it come from?
- Does the information come solely from the transaction system being investigated or is there need to access information produced elsewhere, perhaps outside the organization?
- How should the data be processed in order to provide the decision support system?

● How does the user need to have the information presented for optimal use?

The final requirements could be described as *organization-wide requirements*. You must be aware of the fact that the successful taking of an order from a customer will lead to stock being taken out of the warehouse. This will have an effect on the stock recording sub-system. If the quantity of stock of any item falls below a certain level it may trigger off a purchase order, an order which is sent to the supplier so that stock can be replenished.

Similarly, if an order is taken the goods will have to be delivered by van and this may have an effect on the vehicle scheduling system. And your old department, Accounts, will also be affected because an invoice for the goods sent will have to be sent to the customer and details will have to be stored on the sales ledger system.

Hence it is necessary to consider the effects of an activity, or a change in procedures, in one department on the other departments of the organization.

Developing a systems profile

In order to develop a profile of the system under investigation you might use the following checklist of questions:

Volume
● What is the volume of activity?
● What is the frequency of the activity?
● Does the activity occur in a cycle of any type?
Control
● What aspects of the activity are in need of control?
● What methods of control are currently being used?
● How is performance assessed?
● How are mistakes and errors dealt with?
● Is it possible to by-pass the system? If so, how?
Processes
● What are the individual processes which make up the activity?
● What triggers the activity?
● How long does each activity take? What are the constraints upon the time factor?
● What can cause delays?

- What are the forms of interaction with other systems and with the outside world?
- How much does the current system cost to operate?
- What are the management objectives to be satisfied?
- What are the decision-making requirements of the system?

Data

- What transaction data enters the system, and where does it come from?
- In what form is the transactions data received, and how is it stored?
- What data is produced as a result of the transaction, and how is it stored?
- Who uses the information produced by the system, and what for?
- Is there any data produced which is not used, if so, what?
- Is all the transactions data and reference data required present and accurate?
- What reference data is used? Where does it come from?
- What coding systems are used?

Fact-finding techniques – interviewing

Finding out what the system is supposed to do and what it actually does is a long, involved task. We have summarized the main methods of fact finding and their purposes in Figure 4.4.

Questions

4 Who would you go to in order to find out about user requirements and how would you go about collecting the information?
5 How would you go about finding out how the current system works?

Well, in response to question 4, just where would you go for information about user requirements? The answer seems obvious; you would go to the users themselves and find out what they require. A word of advice, note the emphasis of *requirements* rather than wants. If you ask users what they want, they may be tempted to ask for many things they do not need and do not have the time to use.

A further point to note is that interviewing is a time-consuming activity. It will be necessary to limit the number of people you select

Method	Purpose
Interviewing: Structured Unstructured	For standard set of questions, eliciting facts, speed of processing To draw out ideas and opinions
Questionnaires:	Standard set of questions to many respondents or at many sites
Observation:	Working environment, Work patterns, Information use
Record inspection:	Background material information about how the system is supposed to operate document availability and use

Figure 4.4   Fact finding – methods and purposes

for interviewing and ensure that the people you interview have information that you cannot gain by other means.

Having decided to approach the users, you must decide which users to interview, bearing in mind that in Chapter 3 we saw that there were three types of users. The sensible choice would be the indirect users, that is the managers and heads of department who are concerned with what the system is going to produce. It is likely that the head of Sales and Marketing, Charles Ongar, will be able to outline what he sees as the main *strategic* requirements of the system. This is a good place to start, because you will be able to see the place of the telephone orders system within the context of the overall requirements of the organization.

Your next source of information would probably be the manager of the Sales Department, Sally Gee, who would be able to tell you what she sees as the major *operational* requirements of the system. Furthermore, she will be able to outline the limitations and defects of the existing system.

Note that we have suggested that you approach the indirect users first, although the list of requirements given above listed the transactions elements before the decision-based ones. This is quite deliberate and is part of the top-down approach that is generally recommended. You start at the top with general requirements and work down to the finer detail. Another reason is that you will need to have the managers introduce you to the relevant direct users; hence the need to approach them first. Besides which, it is a matter of courtesy.

The technique that you would use to elicit information is known as *interviewing*. This is a method whereby information is collected verbally through questions being asked. Two points must be made right at the outset.

1 An interview is not an interrogation, it is an exchange of information.
2 The questions must be asked of the appropriate people. There is no point in asking the orders clerk about company policy and intentions, just as the head of Sales and Marketing will almost certainly not have knowledge of the day-to-day operational problems of handling telephone orders.

Structured and unstructured interviews

Having decided to interview users, you must decide what form the interview will take. A *structured* interview is one in which you, the interviewer, use standardized questions. But for your interviews with the head of Sales and Marketing you may prefer to use an *unstructured* interview. Here the method allows for the free flow of ideas and is more suited to situations where you wish to get ideas from the respondent. Such an interview does not take much time to set up because, while you will want to decide on the areas for discussion in advance, you will not need to prepare the precise wording of your questions.

In general terms, unstructured interviews confer the following advantages:

1 You can be more flexible in the wording of your questions.
2 You can explore topics as and when they arise.
3 They may provide information that you may have overlooked or not been aware of.

But you will find that unstructured interviews have some snags and limitations:

1   You may make it difficult to distinguish fact from opinion.
2   They can represent an inefficient use of time.

When it comes to interviewing the direct users of the system it is more likely that you would employ a structured interview. This provides the following advantages:

1   You use the same wording to questions for all the interviewees.
2   You therefore will find it easier to conduct the interview.
3   Interviews can be shorter than if unstructured.
4   The responses to your questions can be more objective.
5   You require less interviewing skill and experience.

However, structured interviews also have their disadvantages:

1   You need to spend more time preparing them. Therefore they are costlier to prepare than unstructured interviews.
2   You may find it difficult to apply strictly a uniform, structured series of questions.
3   You are likely to find the level of interviewee spontaneity to be low and there is no scope for supplementary questions and comments.

When using a structured interview, you can adopt an *open-response question* format. Here you ask a standard question but allow the interviewee freedom in giving his answer in his own words. This provides some flexibility but can result in more time having to be spent analysing the answers.

The least flexible method of interviewing involves your using *closed-response questions*. Here you would give the interviewee a set of possible answers from which he would choose the most appropriate. In using this format you must allow for the possibility that none of the suggested answers is appropriate.

Conducting an interview

As we said earlier, an interview is not an interrogation, and in a business context you will be more successful if you follow a number of simple rules:

1   Plan the interview well in advance. This, in turn, means that you should:
   ● Make an appointment, especially with senior staff, well before the proposed date of the interview
   ● Explain the purpose of the interview at the time of making the appointment
   ● Limit the time to be spent to one hour.
2   Prepare for the interview by:
   ● Getting to know who the interviewee is in the hierarchy and what he or she does. You can consult your organization chart
   ● Prepare the questions that you are intending to ask.
3   Conduct the interview by:
   ● First introducing yourself and stating the purpose of the interview, which is to elicit information, and the nature of the project you are working on
   ● Start with general questions, before going on to finer detail
   ● Following up issues raised by the interviewee which you may not have previously considered
   ● Limit note-taking in order to avoid distracting the interviewee
   ● At the end of the interview, go over your notes with the interviewee to ensure that there are no misunderstandings and that nothing important has been omitted
   ● Thank the interviewee and mention the possibility of a further interview if required.

You have probably attended interviews, perhaps for a job or for a place at college, so you will understand that the interviewee is likely to find the situation tense. You will find when the role is reversed, that is when you become an interviewer, you will also feel anxious. This is a natural human reaction.

Remember how you felt when being interviewed and show courtesy and expect the interviewee to behave in what may appear to be a strange way. Examples of odd behaviour might include:

1   Trying to guess the answer rather than admit ignorance.
2   Telling you what he thinks you want to hear rather than the facts.
3   Telling you that everything is all right and that change is totally unnecessary.
4   Clearly withholding information and being unco-operative.
5   Moaning about how he is being treated by the firm or his boss.

Fact-finding techniques – questionnaire

So far we have looked at your need to collect information from a limited number of people, perhaps a couple of managers and one or two operatives. You will find that the use of interviews, with its face-to-face contact, is probably the best way of eliciting the information you require.

Questions

6 Suppose you have to ask the same set of questions of a large number of people, how would you go about the task?
7 Who would you select as respondents for a questionnaire?

Question 6 changes the direction of our fact-finding study. If you need to extract similar information from several people, perhaps in several departments or spread over a number of sites, interviewing would take too long and the best solution could be for you to use a *questionnaire*. This is a document which contains a number of standard questions.

Open-ended questionnaires are generally those in which the questions ask for an opinion and allow sufficient space for the respondents to write fairly lengthy answers. If you use open-ended questionnaires you allow respondents not only to give their answers, but also the reasons. This information could be usefully analysed later on.

The alternative is the *closed* questionnaire. Here you would ask questions whose answers would be limited to yes/no, to agree/disagree, or to select one of a range of values. You limit the responses possible, but it is quicker and easier for the respondent and does force the respondent to take a stand or express an opinion.

One feature to note about questionnaires is that anonymity is common. That means that you do not insert questions which would reveal the identity of the respondent. This should result in greater honesty in answering the questions. And the use of standardized questions can also produce more dependable information. But you should also realize that it is common for there to be a low response rate, so if you send out one hundred forms for completion you should not be surprised if you get as few as twenty or thirty responses.

Now let us consider question 7. If there are many potential respondents, it is nevertheless important not to spread questionnaires as though they were confetti simply because the forms have been printed. Inappropriate people may not have the knowledge and understanding to give the answers needed, and because you cannot identify the individual respondents you cannot remove any inappropriate responses.

It is therefore important that you direct the questionnaires to those people who have the appropriate knowledge. For example, if you are investigating the telephone ordering procedures, you would ask questions of those people who are associated with the system, the order clerks and the switchboard operators, and not the accounts clerks.

Developing a questionnaire

Preparing a questionnaire is not simply a matter of putting a few questions onto a piece of paper. Your starting-point must be the purpose of the questionnaire – what are you trying to learn from the results? Good questions, and by that we mean questions with unambiguous wording, can take a long time to develop and will often need refining before they can be incorporated in the document. Guidelines for the preparation of a questionnaire include:

1   Decide beforehand what facts and/or opinions are needed and who can provide them.
2   Select between closed and open-ended questionnaires, and allow for the possibility of having a mixture of the two types.
3   Check for defects in the questions such as:
    ● Repetition of questions
    ● Ambiguous wording
    ● Questions which suggest a preferred answer
    ● Questions that may be interpreted differently as between people with different experience
    ● Jumbled sequencing of questions.

4   Pretest the questionnaire on a small, sample group and analyse the results. This might show up defects which should be corrected.

Fact-finding techniques – observation

The interviews with the manager and the operatives will tell you how the system is supposed to work and what should be happening. The manager will provide an overall view of the system and its procedures; the operatives will tell you what happens and what they actually do.

Questions

8 Having conducted your interviews, is there any way you can verify the accuracy of the information given to you?
9 List the things that you might wish to observe when observing the telephone orders clerks at Ongar Winemart.

In response to question 8, there is only one way for you to verify the statements made to you and that is to observe the system in action.

Let us consider some examples. The manager tells you that orders clerks should be able to handle telephone orders in an average of two minutes; the orders clerks claim that it takes at least three minutes because of the poor response time of the computer system. So you go and observe the clerks at work.

What did you list in response to question 9? A sample list might include some of the following:

● How long does it take to identify the customer
● How much time is spent on 'social' talk
● The time taken to enter an order and, more importantly
● The time taken for the computer to respond to the request
● The time elapse between the clerk putting down the telephone and his having to pick it up again to take the next call
● Whether the clerk mentioned special offers, and if so whether at the beginning of the telephone call or at the end
● Whether the set procedures are always followed.

This list is by no means exhaustive and, no doubt, you would look at some other things as well. It would certainly make sense for you to observe these activities at different times of the day or days of the week in order to confirm your findings. Again we should emphasize that the purpose is not to spy, nor is it to prove anybody right or wrong; it is simply to elicit facts about the actual operation of the system.

Observation might also be relevant to the activities of the senior managers. For example, Charles Ongar might say that as head of the Sales and Marketing unit he receives a particular report about telephoned orders every week. It would be useful to know when he receives it, when he looks at it, what he does with the information. Recipients of information frequently claim to use the information though they may do no more than glance at the front page and then have the document filed, never again to see the light of day.

You will also be able to observe the environment in which the work activities take place. Temperature, humidity, lighting and arrangement of office furniture can all affect work performance. One example we came across, illustrates this point. The company concerned bought goods from a large number of suppliers and the dispatch forms which accompanied the goods were stacked in piles on the floor around a large document reader. Each pile consisted of all the dispatch notes for one day. Staff operating the document reader would tread on the documents, tearing them or making them dirty; or staff would knock over the piles causing documents to be replaced in the wrong pile. As a result of this, purchase ledger staff who had to refer to the documents when the invoices came in for payment would have to spend several minutes wading through the piles of documents searching for the required form.

The example we have given is a true, though extreme, case. But for Ongar Winemart, quite apart from observing how the clerks carried out their tasks, you might observe the placing of the visual display units relative to the clerks' desks, whether the clerks could always gain the information they required from the computer system, whether the clerks had either to refer to written documents or create documents in response to telephone orders, and whether there was supervision of the telephone orders office.

It is essential that you take into account the limitations to observation as a technique of fact finding. In particular, you will find that people tend to adjust their manner and speed of working simply because they are being watched. This could distort your view of the operation of the system. In order to understand more fully the system, it might be useful for you to engage in *participant observation*, that is actually to do the job of work concerned. This would provide another perspective to your fact finding.

Fact-finding techniques – record inspection

You will find that the organization has a great deal of information that will be useful. We have already looked at the possibility of using or creating organization charts and the value of looking at the annual report. Now we will consider record inspection as part of the formal fact-finding activity.

The company should have, for example, a *user guide* or manual for the system you are investigating. This details the inputs, processes and outputs of the system. The document will show you how the system ought to be carried out and the associated forms and documents. Your interviews with the operations staff and your observations should show whether the system has to be altered.

Similarly, you could inspect the documents used by the system to see whether there is any difference between the intended use and actual use. Further, you could collect samples of all the documents which should be used and a separate set of samples of all the documents that are used to see whether there is redundancy of forms or whether unofficial new forms have been introduced into the system.

It is important, though, that you cross-check the documents with facts as collected through other means in order to understand fully what is happening.

Determining user requirements

You have collected as many facts as you can about the telephone orders system, and the users have told you what they need. How do you go about determining what is wanted and presenting your findings in a way that is clear to the users?

Question

10 List the general problems you are likely to face when trying to determine user requirements.

There are several problems that you will face as an analyst:

1   You need to be able to see the requirement through the user's eyes. A manager tends to be a *doer* rather than an *explainer*, often doing things intuitively. He may not have the ability to convey in detail what he needs, and you will not know unless he tells you.
2   There is a danger that you might get overwhelmed with detail and therefore you need to be able to organize the details, using them as required.
3   In designing a new system, you are likely to produce a detailed specification. But this is a technical document that would be of greater use to computer specialists than to the more 'generalist' manager. On the other hand, if you write a generalized document that makes sense to the users it is possible that the technical content will be inadequate.

Data flow analysis

One approach that you can use is *data flow analysis*. This is a method whereby we can study the use of data in each activity. We can draw *data flow diagrams* to show, visually, where data originates, how it is processed, and what happens to it.

Let us consider Ongar Winemart's new system. This will:

1   Enable customers to telephone in their orders.
2   Give clerks rapid access to computer files to verify that the company has the required, or substitute, stock available and be able to advise customers of special offers.
3   Create a file of orders to be delivered.
4   Enable lists of next day's deliveries to be printed and sent to the warehouse for action.
5   Update the sales ledger with invoices for goods dispatched.

Let us now draw a simple data flow diagram covering the overall general requirement. This is shown in Figure 4.5. The notation we use is very simple, and consists of four symbols:

● Double   Source or destination of data. This
   square   represents external sources or
               destinations

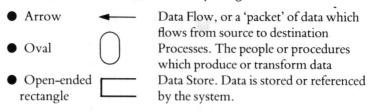

- Arrow — Data Flow, or a 'packet' of data which flows from source to destination
- Oval — Processes. The people or procedures which produce or transform data
- Open-ended rectangle — Data Store. Data is stored or referenced by the system.

We give each component in a data flow diagram a suitable description. Note that we have not made any assumptions about use of a computer system; the emphasis is very much on what happens to the data.

We need to be aware that the data flow diagram is a representation of the *logical* activities. That is, it tells us *what* is happening to data, and *when*. It is not concerned with *physical* features.

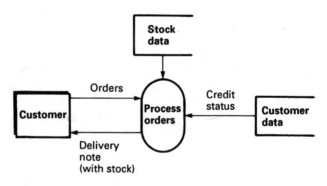

Figure 4.5   A simple data flow diagram

Figure 4.5 clearly is of limited value. It simply shows that information flows between the organization and the customer. In this case, orders are received from the customer; delivery notes are sent to the customer. The activity involved in processing the order. And in order to do so, there is need to make use of two stores of data: stock data and customer data.

We clearly need to expand and label more clearly the data flow diagram if we are to make any sense of the system. This we see in Figure 4.6. What we have done here has been to show more clearly how we verify that the order is valid. We have also indicated the resulting flow of information from the acceptance of the order. Hence

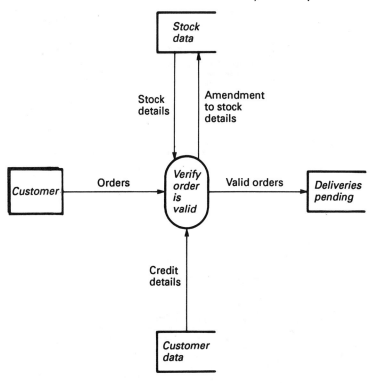

Figure 4.6   A flow diagram expanded further in order to show delivery
notes and update sales ledger data files

we see the creation of a new data store, that relating to deliveries
pending.

Figure 4.6 is still rather limited in that it deals only with the data
flow as it pertains to the Telephone Orders Section. It tells us that
customers' orders are verified for validity and, if valid, placed in a data
store known as Deliveries Pending. The system must be expanded
further so that the deliveries pending data store creates delivery notes
which go to the customer; further, it must update further sales ledger
data files to reflect the increasing indebtedness of customers. Such
expansion is seen in Figure 4.7.

Here we introduce two further activities. First, the assembly of the
delivery schedule. Because deliveries are made to customers only on

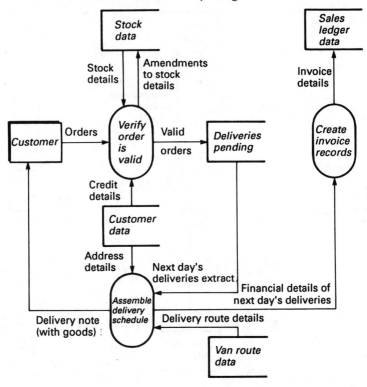

Figure 4.7 An expanded data flow diagram showing the flow of information from the acceptance of the order

specific days of the week, we need to extract the relevant information from:

1 The deliveries pending data store. This tells us which customers require deliveries to be made.
2 The van route data store, which tells us the geographic areas to which deliveries will be made on a specific day.

We use this activity to create the delivery note. The activity serves another purpose. We must ensure that each movement of goods has a corresponding movement of money. So, the activity of assembling the delivery schedule creates a further flow of information. This is the financial information which flows into our second new activity; the

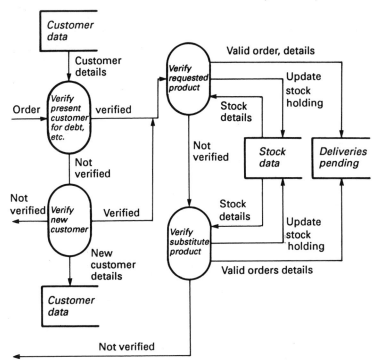

Figure 4.8   Detailed flow diagram to show how customer information is verified

creation of invoice records. This activity, in turn, moves the new financial information to the sales ledger data store.

We are sure that you have noticed that there has been no mention of error conditions. For example, we have made no mention of what happens if the customer has many bills outstanding or if the goods required are not available. This does not mean that we ignore these conditions; of course we must. But these can be treated at a lower level of data flow diagram. At this overall level we do not want the diagram excessively cluttered with detail.

Figure 4.8, as you can see, is much more detailed. This shows how we verify the customer information which accompanies the order. Only when the customer is accepted do we verify the products ordered. Thus the orders information goes through a number of checking stages before the information finally flows into the deliveries pending data store.

The main advantages of using data flow diagrams stem from their simplicity. Users as well as systems analysts can understand them. As a result, users can get more involved in describing and, ultimately, in the design of the system.

Developing data flow diagrams

Question

11 If you have an application to develop, such as the telephone ordering system, how would you go about constructing a series of data flow diagrams?

The answer to question 11 is hinted at above. There is no reason why you should not draw several levels of data flow diagram. The method that is commonly adopted is known as *top-down*.

That is, you would start with a diagram that shows the basic flows of data at an overall level, as in Figure 4.5. This can be *exploded* as in Figure 4.7 to show the stages undergone at the next level down. You could draw data flow diagrams at the next level down to show, for example, the detailed procedures for verifying that the order is valid. This is shown in Figure 4.8.

Here we see that when an order comes in, the first step is to verify that the customer is an existing one who is not excessively in debt to the company. If not, then the customer is verified for acceptability as a new one. If the customer is acceptable, then it is possible to go to verify the requested product. If it is not in stock then a substitute is verified. If a product is ordered, then the product data is updated to ensure that there are no attempts to sell stock that has been allocated and the deliveries pending data is updated with the details of the customer and his order.

You can, if you wish, take any of the stages in the verification process and explode the activity still further to the next stage down.

Data dictionary

Data flow diagrams are all very well as a means of describing the flow of data, but they are not sufficient to describe the data fully. In our diagrams we referred to 'stock data' and 'customer data', but what data are these? Do we all agree on all of the constituent data elements? And even if we do agree on the required contents, do we all use the same names?

A properly developed *data dictionary* should eliminate these problems, because it is a list of all the data elements and their details included in the data flow diagrams which are used to describe a system.

As you will see shortly, a data dictionary is a formal statement of the data elements used in the system and how they relate to one another. It therefore represents a *logical* relationship. This is later refined in the design of the data file system which shows how data elements are related in a *physical* manner.

All the data in a system consists of *data elements*; these are known variously as *fields* or *data items* and are the smallest units of meaningful information. Examples of data elements might include the product's stock reference number, its price, or its description.

A group of data elements that are associated with one another is known as a *data structure*. For example, there might be a logical data structure called *stock* which consists of all the data elements in the stock data store.

Questions

12 Describe the relationship between data flows, data stores, data structures and data elements.
13 List the contents of the stock data store.

We have seen how data flow diagrams use data stores, so let us try to answer Question 12 by formalizing the relationship between these various references to 'data'. Gane and Sarson in their book Structured Systems Analysis defined the relationship very simply indeed.

'Data flows are data structures in motion; data stores are data structures at rest.'

They showed the data description hierarchy diagrammatically as:

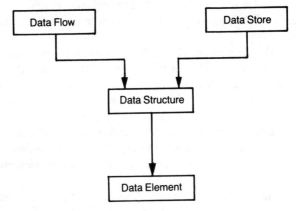

Figure 4.9

In your answer to Question 13 we would expect you to have most of the following data elements:

Stock reference details:
- Stock reference number
- Stock item description
- Stock item pack size
- Stock item supplier code
- Free stock (alias quantity in hand)
- Allocated stock (alias quantity allocated)
- Re-order level
- Re-order quantity
- Purchase order quantity outstanding.

Some of the elements we listed above will not be used as part of the formal telephone orders system but nevertheless are part of the stock data structure. It is likely that other data elements will be included such as date of last purchase order.

Describing data elements

The minimum information we need for describing a data element for the data dictionary is its name and description. In practice, further information is required if the system is to be fully understood.

A more formal list of information is as follows:

1   *Data name*. This is a unique name which is used to describe the data element. Common words such as '*date*' should be avoided as they could be ambiguous; for example, does it mean order date, delivery date, invoice date, etc.? Far better to use something like *order-date* or *date-of-order*.

2   *Data description*. This should be a brief outline of the meaning of the data element, and may include an example.

3   *Alias*. This is an additional name by which the data element may be known. In the stock example above, *free stock* is also known as *quantity in hand*. It is vital that the data dictionary includes all aliases.

4   *Data values*. There are two types of value that a data element can take. First, those which can be any value within a range. An example might be the value of a transaction which might range from zero to £99,999.99. This is known as a *continuous* data element.

Secondly, codes which might have certain particular values. For example, sex may be coded as 'F' or 'M'. Here the code has some meaning and is known as a *discrete* data element. It is important that the data dictionary contains the relevant table which provides all the possible meanings of the values of the code.

It is important that the dictionary includes any information that might be relevant on the possible range of values because this will be used in the design of controls for the system.

5   *Length*. You will need to specify the length in characters of each data element.

6   *Encoding*. If the data element is to be encoded in a special way, such as packed decimal or binary coded decimal, you should specify this in the data dictionary.

You will find that a data dictionary has uses quite apart from the determination of user requirements. It can also act as a common source of definitions to users and analysts. And the very act of compiling a dictionary forces the analysts to clarify their understanding of the data and its uses. Any cross–referencing should reveal different processes which share common data; it should also reveal redundant data elements.

Assignment 4

Select a local business and for that business prepare:
(a) a data flow diagram, and
(b) a data dictionary of its purchasing system.

Recap

In determining systems requirements, you have to engage in a *fact-finding* exercise. The methods of fact finding are:

● *Interviewing*, where you speak to and question users directly about the existing system and their needs from the new one. These may be *structured*, where you stick to a rigid set of pre-prepared questions, or *unstructured*, where you allow the interview to flow but may find irrelevances introduced
● *Questionnaires*, which are most commonly used where you seek to have the same questions answered by several people, perhaps with their own special perspectives
● *Observation*, which is used to verify information given in interviews and also enables you to see what actually happens as against what you are told should happen
● *Record inspection*, in which you examine documented information about the organization, such as *organization charts*, and *company reports*, or the documents used in or produced by the system.

A particularly useful tool to use for analysing the system is the *data flow diagram*. This attempts to show in a pictorial manner the network of data flows between external bodies and internal storage and its processing. These can be prepared at a number of different levels, using a *top-down* approach so that the highest levels show the broad outline of the system, while the details are shown at the lower levels.

Complementary to data flow diagrams is the *data dictionary* which describes, in detail, all the data elements which are referenced in the diagrams.

Answers

1 You will need to collect as much background information as possible. This will include the organization, structure.

2 There are 4 main headings:
- Basic requirements
- User transactions requirements
- User decision requirements
- Organization-wide requirements

3 Basic requirements:
- The basic business process
- Data used and produced during the process
- The limitations imposed by time and volume of work
- Performance controls

User transactions requirements:
- Well structured
- Activities are frequent and predictable
- Highly structured data requirements
- Concerned with current events with an emphasis on detail

User decision requirements:
- Not routine
- Occur irregularly and less predictable
- Determined by the individual
- Often compares today's results with yesterday's
- Broad view, based on summary data

Organization-wide requirements:
- Effects on other systems within the organization

4 You would go to the users, normally conducting an interview.

5 The department manager should be able to tell you how the system is intended to work. The operatives will be able to tell you what actually happens.

6 You would employ a questionnaire.

7 You would select only those people who have appropriate knowledge.

8 You can use observation. Or you can cross-check against information supplied by other interviewees.

9
- How long it takes to identify the customer
- How much time is spent on 'social' talk
- The time taken to enter an order
- The time taken for the computer to respond to the request
- The time elapse between the clerk putting down the telephone and his having to pick it up again to take the next call

- Whether the clerk mentioned special offers, and if so whether at the beginning of the telephone call or at the end
- Whether the set procedures are always followed

10
- The manager may be poor at explaining his or her needs
- You may receive too much detail
- Producing a document pitched at a level suitable for both the technical expert and the user

11 You should use a 'top-down approach. In this, you would define the flows at a broad level. Then you would define each of the broad activities in greater detail.

12 These have been defined as 'data flows are data structures in motion; data stores are data structures at rest'. A data structure is a combination of data elements or fields.

13
- Stock reference number
- Stock item description
- Stock item pack size
- Stock item supplier code
- Free stock (alias quantity in hand)
- Allocated stock (alias quantity allocated)
- Re-order level
- Re-order quantity
- Purchase order quantity outstanding.

5: Systems design

Objectives

After reading this chapter, you should be able to:

- Explain how we decide on the design of the business information which comes out of the computer
- Outline the importance of time considerations and user-friendliness
- Explain what information needs to be entered into a system and how the information should be validated
- Explain the ways in which data may be stored in a computer system for rapid and accurate processing
- Outline what is entailed in devising methods to ensure that data is held securely
- Describe data control methods
- Describe the need for a proper specification for the purchase of an applications package.

Scenario

You are still working at Ongar Winemart as a systems analyst and have completed your analysis of the telephone orders systems using the techniques as outlined in Chapter 4.

You are now required to design a new system which will enable customers' telephoned orders to be processed quickly, meet the requirement that the clerks act as sales-people rather than mere takers of orders, provide links with the stock recording and sales ledger systems and provide various pieces of management information.

Phases of systems design

The design process takes place at two levels:

1 *Logical design*, which is that part of the design process where you
   write the detailed specification of the new system.
2 *Physical design*, namely the activities involved when you turn the
   logical design into a reality.

Questions

1 List the features that you would expect to find in the logical design of
   Ongar Winemart's telephone orders system.
2 In what sequence would you expect to undertake the logical design of
   the system?

Consider your answer to question 1. This, quite simply and in brief,
should be:

1 Outputs to be produced by the system.
2 Data inputs to the system.
3 The file structure.
4 The procedures to be carried out, whether by computer or by
   human operative.

Attempting to answer 2 is far more difficult. But let us give the matter
some thought. Chapter 4 was concerned with the issue of *user
requirements*. This should give us a clue to your starting-point, at least.
Outputs from the system are the prime purpose in having a system.
As far as the telephone orders system is concerned, the purposes of the
system are:

1 To enable customers to get the goods they ordered.
2 To have the warehouse know what to pack ready for delivery.
3 To enable correct invoices to be sent to customers.
4 To facilitate the keeping of accurate records of customers'
   accounts.
5 To allow managers to know the status of individual orders should
   there be an enquiry from a customer.

6 To permit managers to retrieve summary information about orders during a given time period or by customer type, etc.

The other stages really subserve the output requirements. You may decide to consider next the procedural elements, namely the rules whereby the output requirements are met. But you will also need to have designed the logical inputs so that you can relate the rules to those inputs, and you will find the need for file design to be considered, too.

Design of the outputs from the system

This, as mentioned previously, must be the first stage in the logical design. Essentially, this is about the *presentation of information.*

Questions

3 What are the key issues that need to be considered by the systems analyst when designing outputs?
4 List the main features of printed output and paper as a medium of output.

In answering question 3, five issues immediately come to mind when considering the design of output:

1 *The recipient of the output.* There is no point in producing output that is not going to be used; so the starting-point must be the intended user. Within this we might distinguish between users on the following bases:
   ● *Internal or external user.* The presentation of information is likely to differ depending upon whether the information goes outside the organization or whether it remains inside. Outside bodies may have specific requirements, for example suppliers may insist that orders are placed on documents prepared to a specific format, or the Inland Revenue requires end-of-year tax returns in a distinct layout. Internal needs are not always that definitive
   ● *Rank in the organizational hierarchy.* For internal documents you must bear in mind that the greater the person's importance within the organization the less detail they want. The company

director will not want, and does not have the time, to examine and digest the mass of details pertaining to individual orders from customers. He or she will be interested in overall figures and trends; the operative has far greater need for detail.

2   *The intended use of the information.* There are three main uses to which information is put and these will determine the contents, style of presentation and medium used:

- *Provision of knowledge.* This is mainly about what has happened in the past. Examples would include an analysis of sales to customers or a list of products and their quantities in the warehouse

- *Request a response,* for example an invoice which goes out to a customer will ask the customer to respond by paying within a certain number of days. A response is sometimes best facilitated by use of a 'tear-off' strip, such as a remittance advice which is a piece of paper attached to the invoice and has all the essential information for the company to be able to process the accompanying cheque.

- *Trigger an action,* where the intention is to bring information to the attention of somebody with the power to take remedial action. This might be an internal document such as a bin ticket used in the company's stores which warns that the factory is now beginning to use reserve, safety stock and that there is an urgent need to re-order from the supplier. It might be a document which goes outside the organization, such as a warning letter to a customer that payment is long overdue and that legal action will be taken to recover the debt unless it is paid immediately.

3   *Quantity of detail required.* This, as mentioned earlier, will often depend upon who is to receive the information. You often have greater scope for imaginative design forms when there is little information to convey; but large detailed listings, such as price lists, tend to be more straightforward. The quantity of detail may, in turn, affect the medium that you will use especially in the light of time considerations.

4   *Time considerations.* These will include:

- *Permanent or transient requirements.* The basic issue that you have to consider here is whether the information that is presented is needed for a very short period of time. An example might be stock availability during a customer's telephone enquiry. Or whether the information needs to be readily available for long enough to be worth printing onto paper and storing in a filing cabinet

- *Frequency of output.* You may design output documents depending upon how often they need to be produced and in what quantities. This may also affect whether multi-part set documents are produced or whether single copies are produced.

5   *Available methods of output.* There are three output media:

- You would use *printed output* for information that is intended to go outside the organization, for long lists that cannot easily be handled in any other way, and for information that is needed for long periods of time or needs to be referred to frequently
- *Displayed output* on a VDU is best suited to transient information, where there is short-term, two-way communication with the computer system. This is often associated with interrogation of the central database
- *Spoken output* through synthetic sound is becoming more common. A number of banks have introduced home banking systems, where the account holder dials the computer's telephone number and the computer generates spoken instructions and information.

Major features of printed output and paper as a medium

Question 4 is concerned with how you as a systems analyst view output based on the use of paper. Most of you, if not all, will have received some printed output produced by a computer system.

Look at a bank statement you have received recently. This will have your name and address printed at the top of the page, and is followed by a single line for each transaction showing the date, the transaction type, value, and the balance outstanding. Or examine a bill from the electricity board. This will have very little information actually printed by the computer, merely your name and address, account number, date and how much you owe. It will also have a tear-off strip with some of the printed information duplicated to be returned with your payment.

Both of the above examples are documents which have gone outside the organization, the bank statement simply provides information, though it may suggest that remedial action is required if you are overdrawn, and the electricity bill quite positively requires a response.

You will no doubt have noticed that the computer-produced documents were of different sizes and may have used colours differently. Computer printers can print documents of almost any size up to about 15 inches wide, depending upon the type of printer being used. But there are certain standard *stock sizes* of paper, 9.5 inches wide by 11 inches deep being one commonly used size. The paper itself comes in *continuous* or *fanfold* form with a perforation between each sheet and sprocket holes at regular intervals down each side of the paper for guiding the paper through the printer's paper-feeding mechanism.

The paper may be in single part. Multi-part sets are used where two or more copies of the same document are required, for example one going to the customer and the other being retained for the record at head office. Where multi-part sets are used it is common for the parts to be interleaved with continuous carbon paper, though some organizations prefer to use *no carbon required (NCR)* paper, in which a chemical on the back of the sheet of paper enables a copy to be made onto the facing sheet.

The use of continuous paper, especially where multi-part sets are used, implies the requirement for form-handling equipment. You can use devices such as *bursters* and *guillotines* to separate the individual sheets, while *decollators* are used to split multi-part sets and cleanly remove the continuous carbon paper. These machines will also trim the sides of the forms to remove the sprocket holes. In this way, the documents you receive from the bank or the electricity board will look very different from the mass of paper from which they originated.

You will also have noticed how the documents will have standard company letter-headings and other regular information. Often this information appears on the document in a colour other than the standard black. This is because it is pre-printed. That is, the company will order forms from their suppliers which have as much standard information printed on them as is possible. This facilitates a fine, prestigious appearance; and, just as important, it reduces the amount of computer printing to a minimum, consisting only of non-standard information. Of course, the cost of pre-printed forms is greater than standard white paper, but the benefits outweigh the extra cost.

You would, in designing the outputs from the system, need to consider when pre-printed forms must or should be used, and when they are unnecessary. Virtually all documents going outside the organization should be pre-printed with the company name and other standard headings. Internal documents will not normally have this requirement.

We have already alluded to a possible requirement to evoke a response from the customer. Let us consider this further. Some output documents act as *turn-round* documents. The electricity bill mentioned earlier is an excellent example of this. The computer repeats the print of your essential account details, reference number and amount of money due, on the detachable remittance advice portion of the bill. After you pay the bill, the remittance advice can be fed through a document reader which reads your account number and posts the amount to your account.

Designing the output layout

By layout we mean the arrangement of headings and details on the output document, whatever the medium used. No matter whether you design a paper document or a transient output onto a VDU, the purpose is to inform, and this requires clarity.

Question

5 List the general rules that you would expect to govern the design of the layout of an output document.

Designing the print layout

Let us consider first some of the general rules associated with designing printed output. Figure 5.1 shows a typical layout for an invoice. In this case the document can be divided into three main parts:

1 *Identification and headings.* At the top of the form you place the company name, control information such as the date and the invoice number, and the identity of the document type.
2 *Detail.* This is the central part of the document where you place the details of transactions.
3 *Totals and messages.* These are placed at the foot of the document.

Ongar Winemart LTD.

47 High Road, High Ongar, Essex.

Invoice

Invoice
Number 27431

Date 08/02/89

To: Greenhills Social Club
Roding Road
Chelmsford CM3 4XJ

Customer G2748
Number

Stock number	Quantity	Unit price	Description	Value
A314	10	7.42	Beggs light ale – 24s	74.20
A497	4	15.60	Hansheim lager – Kegs	62.40
F112	5	1.89	Wine – Jacques D'or White	9.45
F113	4	1.89	Wine – Jacques D'or Red	7.56
M326	3	1.67	Wine – Bulgarian Reisling	5.01
S242	2	9.30	Vladimir Vodka – Litre	18.60
S484	1	9.50	Barnardi Rum	9.50
S768	1	10.45	Glenglen Whisky	10.45
S826	1	11.36	Dollinger Old rye	11.36
X342	8	1.30	Runwald's Crisps Assd	10.40
X348	5	1.14	Salted Peanuts	5.70

Terms:

Payment due in full by 08/03/89

Total 224.63

Vat 33.69

Please
pay 258.32

Figure 5.1   A typical layout for an invoice

The general guidelines which you should follow are:

1   The document should read *left to right* and *top to bottom.*
2   The most important data elements should be the easiest to find –
normally at the extreme left or right, or perhaps enclosed in a box.
3   The document should be titled and, if appropriate, have page
numbers.
4   If you use columns, they should be labelled and be separated by
lines.

5 Labels and titles should be written in full and not in abbreviated form.

6 It should not be crammed with information.

7 It should not have large blank areas.

Designing the VDU screen layout

Many of the principles mentioned above in relation to designing printed output apply to VDU screen output also. Figure 5.2 shows a layout that might be used for interrogating the system to see the contents of an order.

Here the screen area is divided into two distinct areas. The first consists of the *permitted zone* into which the user can write. The example contains two such zones. One is near the top of the screen into which the user enters the customer's account number, and the other is at the foot of the screen and is used to tell the system what the user wants to do next. This is either to exit from the program, or make further inquiries into customers' orders.

```
              Orders Inquiries

  Customer ]G2748[      GREENHILLS SOCIAL CLUB

  STOCK                 UNIT
  NUMBER    QUANTITY    PRICE    DESCRIPTION              VALUE

   A314        10        7.42    BEGGS LIGHT ALE - 24S     74.20
   A497         4       15.60    HANSHEIM LAGER - KEGS     62.40
   F112         5        1.89    WINE - JACQUES D'OR WHITE  9.45
   F113         4        1.89    WINE - JACQUES D'OR RED    7.56
   M326         3        1.67    WINE - BULGARIAN REISLING  5.01
   S242         2        9.30    VLADIMIR VODKA - LITRE    18.60
   S484         1        9.50    BARNARDI RUM               9.50
   S768         1       10.45    GLENGLEN WHISKY           10.45
   S826         1       11.36    DOLLINGER OLD RYE         11.36
   X342         8        1.30    RUNWALD'S CRISPS ASSD     10.40
   X348         5        1.14    SALTED PEANUTS             5.70

  TOTAL                                                   224.63

  PRESS 'E' TO EXIT
        'I' FOR FURTHER INQUIRIES     ] [
```

Figure 5.2   A possible layout for interrogating the system to see the contents of an order

The bulk of the screen area is *protected*, that is, it cannot be written on as it contains information required by the user. On entering the customer's account number, the computer should respond with the customer name and then display the required information. When there is no further information to display, the user must be given the opportunity to clear the screen and use it for some other purpose. Hence the message at the bottom which prompts the user into choosing the next action.

If you want to highlight information, the VDU screen can facilitate this in one of several ways such as through the intensity of the display, the use of inverse video or the use of flashing characters or of different colours.

Most VDU screens are limited to 24 lines of up to 80 characters per line. It is important that information is not crammed into this limited space, and it may be necessary to divide the information which is required by the users over two or more screen displays, allowing the user to move onto the next screen when he or she is ready to do so.

Design of computer input

Good input design is of vital importance to the success of the system. Its importance can be seen in the fact that the capturing and input of data generally accounts for over a quarter of the total costs of a system during its normal lifespan. The problem is that people often get things wrong. Therefore systems analysts do their best to devise simple methods of data input based, as far as possible, upon automatic methods.

Questions

6 What would you regard as the main objectives of input design for the telephone orders system at Ongar Winemart?
7 Why are those objectives so important, and what are they intended to overcome?
8 What data in the telephone orders system do we need to capture?

Most experts would suggest that, in response to question 6, there are five main underlying objectives of input design:

1 *Controlling the quantity of input data.* Succinctly put, the greater the

quantity of data the greater the scope for errors to occur and the longer it will take to enter the data. The implication is simple, you should only input *necessary* data. As we shall see later, the telephone order system would require at best that you enter the customer's identification code number rather than the full name and address; similarly, you would be better off entering the code numbers of the required products rather than their descriptions.

2 *Avoiding delays in data entry.* While you are particularly interested in the output that the system produces, nevertheless the system cannot produce output until after the data has been entered. You cannot dispatch goods to your customers until after their orders have been taken and entered. You cannot send out the invoices until later on. And you will not be paid until some time after the invoices have been received by your customers. Delays therefore cost money. And if your customers are unhappy with the speed of processing their orders they may take their custom elsewhere. That, too, is expensive.

For some purposes, a turn-round document as illustrated by an electricity bill as mentioned earlier is one way of overcoming the difficulty. This would apply especially if the document can be read and therefore entered directly into the system.

3 *Minimizing the number of steps.* The fewer the stages that data goes through before it is finally assimilated the less likely it is that it will be erroneous. Furthermore, it will help save time. At Ongar Winemart, direct entry through the VDU with immediate file update would seem to provide you with the best solution.

4 *Avoiding errors.* As an objective this is paramount. GIGO – 'garbage in, garbage out'. The objectives previously listed are objectives in their own right, but also subserve this one.

5 *Simplicity.* This, too, helps with the avoidance of errors and is more likely to be accepted than a highly complex method. Most staff want a system which enables them to complete their work as quickly as possible; complexity of procedures, especially those involving human action, militates against this.

Now let us consider your answer to question 8. From what we have said up to this point, it should be clear that two types of transaction data must be captured:

1 *Identification data.* You can recognize the customer by his identification code. Similarly, you recognize the products ordered

by the customer by their codes. These codes are sometimes known as the identifying *keys*.

2   *Variable data*. This is when the transactions information varies. For example, in the telephone orders system, the variable data will be the quantity of the product.

Thus the transactions data that needs to be entered can be summarized as *who* wants *how much* of *what*.

By the same token we can see what data *not* to enter:

1   *Details that are readily available*. For example, the customer's name and address are stored in a reference file. There are three reasons why you should not enter these details when transactions are made:
   ● It takes time to enter the information
   ● They would occupy disk storage space unnecessarily
   ● They may be entered incorrectly.

2   *Data that is constant*. The date of the transaction, for example, will be the same for all entries made on a given day. The computer system can have the current date stored internally; this information is readily available.

3   *Details that can be calculated*. For example, to calculate the value of a transaction is easy. The formula you use is

Validation of input

$$Quantity \times Price = Value$$

Quantity   is a variable which must be entered
Price   can be extracted from a data file and is not entered
Value   can be calculated and therefore is not entered

So now you can see that the amount of information that needs to be *entered* into the system for any transaction is far less than the information *relevant* to it.

Question

9 List the things you can do to ensure that the data you have entered is correct.

Question 9 is a vital one. The data held in the system will be no better or more accurate than that which you have entered. We will have more to say about controlling data input a little later on. But for the moment it will suffice to make the point that you must ensure that:

1 The transaction enters the appropriate system. For example, you must take care not to confuse orders *from* customers with orders *to* suppliers or payment *from* customers with payment *to* suppliers.

2 The transaction is *complete*, meaning that every data element that should be present is indeed present.

3 The transaction is *authorized*. This may require that you introduce some form of human control or override. For example, the company may decide that an order will not be accepted from a customer who has exceeded his credit limit. This provides authority to accept an order from a customer who has not exceeded his credit limit.

The points made above are general principles. There may be other, specific, checks that can be made. There are, as we mentioned earlier, two types of transaction data that must be entered. So let us see how these might be validated.

First, identification data such as the customer code or product code. The simplest form of test is to see whether the code *exists* in the appropriate reference file. As the order clerk enters the customer code number, the computer system can look up a customer file using the code number as a key. If a matching record is found, then the corresponding name and address details can be displayed on the VDU screen. If there is no match, then an error message can be displayed in highlighted form. Equally, of course, there should not be a matching record for a new customer whose details will not have been entered.

Secondly, the variable transactions data. Your tests for the quantity of a product might be based on the notion of an acceptable range of possible values. It may be decided that an order for 1000 cases of whisky, with 12 bottles per case, is outside the normal range.

The design of the data filing methods

File organization and processing is central to business computing systems. This must be done in an orderly manner to minimize the amount of storage medium used and to facilitate speedy and correct access to the required data.

At this point it might be useful to remind ourselves of the main elements and constructions of data stored on computer storage media. As we explained in Chapter 2, the smallest piece of useful information is known as a *field*, or *data item*, or *data element*. This might be a surname, colour code, price, quantity, etc.

Fields are physically grouped together to form a *record*, which is the basic block of information handled in a business computer system. The customer record will contain all the relevant information about a particular customer, e.g. code number, name, address, telephone number, name of contact, credit limit, etc.

The record is thus composed of several fields, at least one of which is known as the *record key*, which is unique to that record and is the means of access to the record. In a customer file the customer code number will normally be the record key.

Finally, the *file* is a collection of records that are logically related. Hence we may refer to a customer file, which is the collection of all the customer records.

It is likely that when you design the physical data file system, you will take into account the logical relationships as set out in your data dictionary. Thus, in all the examples of files we have used in this book, we have used records which contain data elements which are logically related to one another.

Question

10 List the different types of files you might expect to encounter in a business computer system.

At least two types of files should come to mind immediately. But as we shall see, there are in fact several different types used for different purposes.

1 A *master file* is a collection of records that is central to the day-to-day affairs of the company. For example, the master file in a sales ledger system will provide information concerning money owed to the company, or a payroll master file will contain the latest position regarding pay details of the company's employees. A master file remains useful only so long as it is both accurate and up-to-date. This requires the use of the next type of file.

2   A *transactions file* contains the records of current transactions prior to the update of the relevant master file. It is important to avoid confusion over the word 'transactions'. This is commonly taken to refer to the business activity of buying and selling. But in business computing, a transaction refers to any activity which affects the organization's master files.

3   A *reference file* is a type of master file which contains information which you need to refer to when processing transactions, updating master files, or producing reports. It will normally contain just the record key together with the corresponding descriptive information.

4   A *report file* is sometimes known as a *print-image file* or a *spooler file*. This is a disk file of print-images of lines of a report created as means of overcoming the limitations of both an inadequate number of printers and the relatively slow speed of the printers. Instead of a program hogging a printer and perhaps not driving it at full speed, the lines of print are written at greater speeds on to a disk file for printing later. Use of such files enables the printer to be driven at their full speed.

5   *Archival files* are data files required to be used at a much later date and stored away from the main computer system.

6   *Back-up files* are copies of master and transaction files which are created for security purposes as will be outlined later on.

File storage media

Files are stored on magnetic media. These are two main types:

1   *Magnetic tape* comes in two main forms, either as cassettes as you might use on an audio cassette recorder or on reels. You are probably quite familar with computer programs stored on cassettes and their limitations of speed and capacity. Their main advantages are their cheapness and size, and they tend to be associated with microcomputers, especially of the home variety rather than business computing. However, some manufacturers of large mainframe and minicomputers occasionally distribute some of their software on cassettes.

Reel-to-reel magnetic tape is a very different matter. The reels can hold up to 1000 metres of tape and store over 50 million characters of information. Furthermore, the process of reading and writing records is very much faster than on cassette.

The main limitation of magnetic tape is that it is a *serial* medium. That is you can only retrieve records in the same sequence as that in which they were written. It is not possible to wind a magnetic tape forwards rapidly and immediately find a specific record. However, as reels of magnetic tape are relatively cheap and compact, they are often used to store back-up copies of files.

Many organizations use *tape streamers* to back-up large disk files. These are relatively large cassettes which enable data to be written on them at high speeds. This means that you could copy the contents of a twenty megabyte hard disk in as little as a quarter of an hour.

2   *Magnetic disks* are also known as *direct access storage devices* or *DASD*. There are four basic types:

● First, the *floppy disk*. This is normally a circular piece of magnetized plastic enclosed in a square flexible envelope. It comes in three sizes. The oldest type was eight inches in diameter, but this is now obsolete. Most common is the 5.25 inches size, but this is increasingly being superseded by the 3.5 inches microfloppy disk which is contained in a toughened plastic shell. Floppy disks can store up to 1.5 megabyte (million characters), though the actual capacity will depend upon both the hardware and software on which the disk is to be used

● Secondly, the *Winchester disk*, which is a fixed disk enclosed in an airtight unit. The capacity of this type of disk ranges from 20 to 100 megabytes, and the processing speed is also much greater than that of the floppy disk. Both the floppy disk and the Winchester are most commonly associated with micro-computers.

● Thirdly, there are disk units of far greater size and capacity which are attached to minicomputers and mainframes. These are generally based on the *exchangeable disk pack* or *cartridge*. This type of unit generally has 2, 6 or 11 circular platters of up to 35 cm diameter mounted on a common hub. The mechanism in the disk drive has a series of seek arms which move together, and each arm has two read-write heads attached to it. The consequence of this arrangement is that data on several, up to 20, different tracks is available to the system without the need to move the arm. This group of associated tracks is known as a *cylinder*. Each disk pack can store up to 250 megabytes

- Finally, the very largest computers might use *fixed-head disks*. In such systems there is one head for each data track, thus providing much faster access to data albeit at some expense. The IBM 3380 houses two fixed disk spindles in each unit, providing over 2.5 billion bytes of data. This is the equivalent of the combined capacities of over 500 of the largest exchangeable disk packs.

Methods of file organization and processing

As we mentioned earlier, you will have to choose the most appropriate methods of file organization if the computer system is to function efficiently.

Questions

11 In what sequence is it best to store Ongar Winemart's customer file records?

12 Is it possible to organize data files so as to enable them to be processed in any sequence?

The answer to question 11 is not at all obvious. Let us start with the self-evident first question, namely what do you want to do with the contents of the customer file? Among the things that come immediately to mind are:

1 Looking up the file to see if the customer is an existing one for which you have a record. This is something you would want to do when the customer phones you up with an order.

2 Providing the name and address details which you print on the delivery notes, invoices, etc.

3 Giving you the list of customers to whom statements of account should be sent at the end of each month.

4 Carrying out a mailshot of all customers of a particular type.

It is quite clear from this list that the access requirements will vary. If the customers have codes ranging from 1 to 2000, you would surely not want to tell customer 249 that he is too late because you are dealing with customer 375. No, when dealing with customers' orders you need to be able to have *random access* to specific records because you do not know in which sequence customers will make their telephone calls.

When printing information that goes to customers, it is likely that you would want to access the customers records in record key sequence; in other words you would use *sequential access*.

In this case, the customer code number would act as the *record key*. This is often known as the *primary key*. You may sometimes want to have an alternative sequence. For example, for some analytical purpose you may wish to process the records in geographic area sequence. To do this you would need to store as one of the fields on the record a code number to represent the area. This field could then be designated as a *secondary key*.

So, how can you arrange things so that the data is available as and when you want it and in the correct sequence? The basic type of file organization is known as *sequential*, where records are stored in the order in which they are written and therefore can only be retrieved in that order.

The main way of overcoming the obvious shortcomings of a sequential file is to index the records. This gives you a form of file organization known as *indexed sequential*, and the method of processing is known as *indexed sequential access method* or *ISAM*.

The ISAM method results in two seeks for each record. First to the index, which will indicate where the data record is stored. Then to the actual data record.

There are other methods of file organization which are sometimes used such as *relative file organization* or *self-indexed files*. Here there is some relationship between the record key number and the starting position of the record relative to the physical beginning of the file. This method saves on the space and time taken up by using indexes, but can lead to wasted disk storage space where there are gaps between the record keys.

Business databases

We have explained how using a data dictionary can help you create your physical data files. Indeed, you will often see very quickly that there are logical combinations of data elements which can be used in designing files.

In relatively simple systems it is common to have a number of separate files, such as customer file, products file, etc., each with its own distinct function. A more recent development on computer systems, even on business microcomputers, is to use a *database management system (DBMS)*.

A DBMS will normally have the following characteristics:

1   It is a single collection of all the data used in the organization.
2   Relevant data is easily accessible to appropriate applications.
3   Duplication of data items is minimized.
4   The logical relationships between the data items are pre-defined.
5   Defining the data and their logical relationships is a separate function from applications programming.

The use of data flow analysis and the development of a data dictionary as explained in Chapter 4 are particularly important elements in the creation of a database. This is because the most modern database systems are based on *relational models*. This is where the logical relationships between data elements is more important than where they are placed physically.

Some microcomputer systems, such as dBASE IV, act as a 'half-way' house as far as database systems are concerned. The dBASE IV filing system is based on the notion of discrete files; but it does allow for linkages between the files so as to create the semblance of a relational database system. And as far as applications programming is concerned, dBASE IV is a *fourth generation language (4GL)* system, as will be explained in Chapter 6, and 4GLs are commonly associated with database systems.

Design of data controls and security systems

Control over the organization's data and programs is extremely important. Failure to introduce proper methods could be expensive and even result in disaster.

Questions

13 List the possible security problems that might be found in the information processing environment.
14 What are the problems that you might expect to find in relation to the control and security of data and how might you overcome them?

Let us consider the list that could be compiled in response to question 13. We put *fire* at the top of ours. In March 1987 a fire at the Open University destroyed £500,000 worth of equipment; and advertisements frequently appear in the computer press for fire-proof safes in which disks and tapes may be safely stored. Next on our list comes *flooding*, and this may be caused by fire-fighting equipment! Market research has shown that in the United States fire was the cause of 15% of computer disasters, while water caused another 10%. Next on our list is *power supply problems*. Both power surges and voltage drops can cause a loss of data. You can use surge protecting plugs to help reduce the incidence of such problems.

The aforementioned problems have nothing to do with the programs or the data. But our list must consider them too. *Hacking*, or unauthorized breaking into computer systems, can also be a problem particularly if the hacker is malicious. It has been found that most unauthorized changes to programs and data have been made internally by fraudulent or disgruntled staff.

There is a clear need to devise methods that would ensure that authorized personnel only would have access to the system; and even then only to those parts of the system for which they had responsibility. This could be done through the use of passwords, known only to the user and the computer manager.

We might also consider unnoticed errors in data or bugs in programs which could remain unspotted for several years. Even expensive purchased software is not always free from errors. The trend towards spreadsheet and other programs written for business microcomputers and intended to be used by non-computing experts may exacerbate the problem. Even though the program may be free from error, the layman may incorrectly interpret the instructions and generate his own mistakes.

Question 14 is concerned with data validation. Here we must distinguish between methods of validation in batch systems from those used in on-line systems.

A *batch* system is one in which the transactions are grouped together and processed in batches. An organization might use this type of system to handle payments received from customers. The remittance advice slips accompanying payment are checked manually and, if correct, grouped together in batches of 20–25. Each batch is given a unique number, and the value of the batch of transactions is calculated and entered in the batch header transactions record together with the number of transactions. The computer program then calculates its own batch totals for the transactions. Only if this figure corresponds to the pre-calculated figure will the transactions be accepted.

In addition, the contents of the batch will normally be printed so that there is a record of what transactions had been entered into the system.

Quite apart from checking the batch total information to ensure that no transactions were missing, and equally that none was duplicated, the computer system would have to check the *contents* of each transaction. The types of tests, such as existence tests and range tests, have already been mentioned.

The other type of transactions processing system is known as an *on-line* system. The telephone orders system at Ongar Winemart is an example of such a system. It is likely that all that can be effectively checked are the individual transactions.

However, procedures would have to be introduced to protect against breakdown of the system. *Log files* are often used to store transactions information. If a breakdown should occur, the system would revert to the point at which the last security copy was taken. The transactions stored in the log file would be used to update the master file automatically. All this is part of the recovery process provided by the standard operating system software.

We must also consider the requirement to ensure the integrity of data files. Regular copying of files to ensure adequate back-up is essential. A commonly used method is known as the *Grandfather-father-son* method of file media cycling. The original version of the file is known as the 'grandfather'. When this is updated, it is written to a separate disk, known as the 'father'. If the 'father' should prove faulty, it would be possible to revert to the 'grandfather' version and re-enter the appropriate transactions to create a new 'father'.

At the next update, the 'father' is used as input, and the output is written to a third disk known as the 'son'. In the event of a fault being discovered it would be possible to go back to the 'father' or even the 'grandfather'.

A further method of ensuring that the correct disk is used is to write the file serial number onto a file header record.

Output data needs to be controlled too. In particular, output which goes outside the organization needs to be checked to ensure that it is both correct and sensible. There are many tales of electricity and gas board computers sending out bills for £0.00 and then threatening letters when the bill for zero value was not paid.

Equally important is to check that all the pages of multi-page documents are present and that recipients do not receive documents intended for somebody else.

The subject of data controls and security is an extremely important one. We will be exploring it further in Chapter 7.

Buying packaged software

Chapter 2 has outlined the reasons why companies, both small and large, sometimes opt for purchasing standard packaged software. The main reason, as was explained, is that it is expensive to develop your own special-purpose software solution; application packages are expensive to develop but their cost is recouped from sales of hundreds or even thousands of copies.

The logical design of a system – that is, the showing of the relationships between inputs, files, processes and outputs – is normally followed by the physical design. This entails writing the detailed specifications of the required outputs, and how they are derived from the inputs and files. These specifications are then transformed into software by the programmers.

Question

15 You have carried out your systems study on the proposed introduction of a payroll system. When is it worth developing the programs 'in-house' and when is it worth buying a standard applications package?

Underlying question 15 is the simple question, is it worth your while preparing a physical design for a commonplace type of application? Is it not a case of simply re-inventing the wheel?

The issues raised have to be faced by most organizations undergoing the process of introducing new 'standard' systems, especially those related to accounting functions. For the more unusual application, where there may not be an applications package, it will almost certainly be necessary to develop the software in-house or commission a specialist software house to do the work.

But the application referred to in question 15 is payroll, a system for which there are many packaged solutions. A common mistake is to assume that if your company employs programmers, then it would be cheaper to have them write the programs. This is not always the case. Your programmers may be engaged in writing programs intended to save the company a great deal of expense. Diverting them to a low value application would be a waste of resources.

A further point for you to consider is that payroll seems a nice easy application. In reality, it is an application full of pitfalls for the unwary. It is subject to change, and therefore the programs are continually amended.

So how do you decide? Your starting-point must be the satisfaction of users' requirements. You might investigate several existing packages and see whether their outputs and methods of calculating gross pay, pensions, etc. meet the needs of users. This is quite apart from the need to check that the major statutory deductions, tax and national insurance, are calculated correctly.

Your organization may be a manufacturing company which has some unusual system of basic, overtime and bonus payments system. Or it may want to be able to derive costing analyses from the system. A packaged system which does not allow for such idiosyncrasies clearly will not meet your company's needs.

A packaged solution may fit the company's basic payroll calculation requirements, but there might also be a desire to link the payroll system to other parts of the company's computer system. If the files produced by the package are not compatible with those of the rest of the computer system, again the package will have to be regarded as deficient. Remember the point made in Chapter 2, that the programs and files in packaged software are not intended to be modified by purchasers.

Another major issue is continuing support. Each year the

government makes changes to the tax and national insurance systems. Sometimes, when using a packaged solution, you can easily modify the appropriate tables used by the system. But occasionally the changes are more far-reaching, such as when statutory sick pay and statutory maternity pay were introduced. You need to be assured that the supplier will still exist and be willing and able to provide the necessary modifications.

Setting up the actual system is another requirement. The package should come complete with well–written and indexed user manuals. There should be help available when the system is set up; and a 'hot–line' to answer queries once the system is in operation.

It is likely that training facilities for use of the package will also be required. Several of these points are discussed further in Chapter 9.

Assignment 5

Using a local business that you have selected for a previous assignment

(a) Design a payroll system, showing the relationships between inputs, files, processes and outputs,
(b) List the ways in which you would ensure that the system was secure from error and the consequences of breakdown and illicit activity.

Recap

The design of a business computer system starts with the *determination of users' needs*. This is normally first translated into the design of *outputs* from the system. The design must closely meet the needs of the actual recipient of the information. The more senior the person, the greater the need for brevity and broad summary information.
Output may have any of three main purposes:

● the provision of knowledge
● to request a response
● to trigger an action.

and may take the form of printed, displayed or audio output. Input to the system has five main objectives:

● to control the quantity of input

122

- to avoid delays in input
- minimize the number of steps
- avoiding errors
- simplicity.

and the transactions data that needs to be captured is *identification data* and *variable data*. However, details that are readily available, constant data and results that can be calculated should not be entered.

Once entered in the system, data is stored as files. Files need to be copied regularly to ensure that their contents are not irretrievably lost in the event of a breakdown in the system. Particular attention needs to be paid to matters of security and control. This entails:

- controlling access to the computer
- batching input transactions
- checking individual input transactions for validity
- file media cycling
- checking output for completeness and reasonableness.

There is a need to be aware of the possibility of using pre-written packaged software, particularly for standard accounting applications. However, the requirement of logical systems design, with its emphasis on users' requirements, still remains. The use of such software will, however, eliminate the heavy costs of software writing.

Answers

1.
   - outputs to be produced by the system
   - data inputs to the system
   - the file structure
   - the procedures to be carried out, whether by computer or by human operative.
2. You would normally design the outputs first. This is followed by design of inputs, files and procedures.
3. Who receives the output, what it is intended to be used for, how much detail is required, time considerations, and the available methods of output.
4. Paper provides permanent output. Computers usually produce output onto continuous paper through a sprocket hole form feeding mechanism. Such output will have to be tidied up by means of bursters and decollators. These separate the sheets and split them

into sets, removing the interleaved carbon. The forms are often pre-printed to provide a smarter look and to reduce the amount of computer printing.

5 Divide the document into three main sections. Identification and headings at the top; details in the middle; totals and messages at the bottom.

The document should read from left to right, and top to bottom. The most important data should be easiest to find. Boxes can be used to highlight data. The document should be titled and numbered. Columns should be labelled and separated by narrow vertical lines. Labels and titles should be written in full, not abbreviated. The document should not be crammed, nor have large unfilled areas.

6 Controlling the quantity of input data.
Avoiding delays in data entry.
Minimizing the number of steps.
Avoiding errors.
Simplicity.

7 To keep errors out of the system and to minimize costs of, and delays to, data capture and entry.

8 The identity of the user, and the identities and quantities of the goods they wish to order.

9 That the transaction enters the correct system, is complete and authorized.

10 Master file, transactions file, reference file, report file, archival file and back-up file.

11 In the sequence that makes for the easiest retrieval of the data records. This is probably in customer number sequence. But we can allow for the use of indexing for random access. We can use secondary keys to provide an alternative key sequence.

12 Yes, through indexing. There are also other data structures that allow for this.

13 Fire, water, power supply difficulties, smoke, unauthorized entry.

14 Data input: Missing transactions and duplicated transactions can be overcome through batching. Errors in the identifying code can be overcome through check digit verification or by accessing the reference file. Range tests can be used on quantities and values.

Data files: Wrong version of the file can be overcome through having the program put the generation number on the file header and having the operator entering the required number. Errors on the current master file will require going back to the previous version; this would suggest media cycling.

Data output: sight checking to ensure that it is correct and sensible and all pages are present.

15 Standard applications, usually of an accounting nature, are often better suited to packaged solutions than esoteric one-off problems. There is a need to examine closely whether the packaged solution meets users' requirements, whether it is 'user-friendly', whether there is continuing support.

6: Choosing and using a programming language

Objectives

After reading this chapter, you should be able to:
- Identify the main features of the popular programming languages, and understand when different languages are appropriate
- Describe the special features of a fourth generation language, and the advantages that it can offer
- Outline the use and relevance of expert systems.

Scenario

Imagine you are Director of Management Information Systems for a large company (Conglomerate Plc), responsible for running the mainframe computer and managing a large group of technical staff, as well as advising on the use of various smaller computers throughout the organization. You have to ensure that the various computer systems efficiently provide the information required on all major areas of company activity such as marketing, personnel, accounting and so on. You frequently have to commission software to be written either by your own staff or by external consultants.

How do they decide what language to use for different applications? What guidelines should you give them?

What is a programming language?

A programming language is a language used to instruct a computer to do things. Programming languages are intended to be easy to use, and therefore often look like English, or at least like algebra. However, computers are very dogmatic in what they can do and can't do, and therefore the syntax of computer languages tends to be very rigid.

One major problem is the incredibly large number of programming languages; there are literally thousands of them. Fortunately many of these are little used or obsolete, and others are aimed at specialist applications such as engineering or architecture, which may not concern you. Nevertheless, the two authors of this book reckon to have a good working knowledge of about twenty-five languages between us. In this chapter, we aim to show you through this maze of languages. Fortunately, it is not as complicated as it might seem at first sight; indeed, if you can program well in one language, it is usually easy to learn others.

The main thing to realize is that essentially computers can only perform four tasks:

1 Input (from mouse, keyboard, tape or disk).
2 Calculate (add, subtract, multiply, divide).
3 Compare and branch.
4 Output (to printer, screen, plotter, tape or disk).

Tasks 1, 2 and 4 are facilities that you would expect from a computer. Task 3 (compare and branch) is perhaps less obvious, but all computers have the facility to proceed to a different set of instructions depending on whether two values are equal or not (or alternatively, if one value is greater than the other). Computer programs very often use 'compare and branch', and this is illustrated in the simple example that follows.

Question

1 Splighorn Ltd sell plastic boxes at 10% discount to trade customers on a standard price of £1.20 each, but give 15% discount on orders of over 50 boxes. A computer program is to be written to input the number of boxes ordered, and to calculate the total amount to be charged. Draw a flowchart to show the calculations to be performed.

The flowchart for this example is shown in Figure 6.1. The essential point to realize is that without a 'compare and branch' facility, even this simple program could not be written. The flowchart is designed

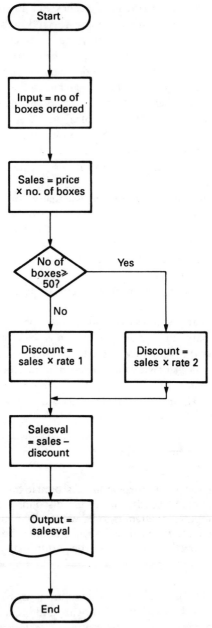

Figure 6.1   Flowchart for calculating quantity discount (Splighorn Ltd)

to show the logic, and is not related to any specific language. It could probably be programmed in any of the languages mentioned in this chapter.

However, although all computer languages are similar in what they do, different languages have particular features which make them more appropriate for certain applications. In the remainder of this chapter, we shall look more at what differentiates the various languages.

Assembly languages

Computers respond to instructions written in binary machine code, which consists just of a string of 1s and 0s such as 1000101. Even the brightest of programmers would find a binary program impossible to get right, so almost all computers can be programmed in an *assembly language* which corresponds directly to machine code. An assembly program consists of a long series of lines of short alphabetic codes such as:

> BRE . A,B   (branch if A & B are equal)

Assembly code is quite unintelligible to anyone who is not an assembly programmer, and it suffers from two major disadvantages:

- it takes a long time to write programs in assembly code, which makes it very costly
- different makes of computer have different assembly codes, so assembly programs are not *portable*: a program written in assembly for one computer must be completely rewritten to run on another computer.

Assembly languages are therefore rarely used for writing applications software. They are quite often used by software houses for coding heavily used routines (such as for data input) in packages. This is because assembly code can be written more efficiently and can run faster than if written in other languages.

Fortunately, there are much better programming languages than assembly for most purposes, but some programs will always have to be written in assembly language or machine code. Other languages need to be translated into machine code for the computer to understand, and this requires a program called a *compiler* (see next section) which has to be written in assembly or machine code.

High-level languages

High-level languages were developed mainly in the 1960s and have evolved since then. They are often now described as *third generation languages*, in order to distinguish them from the more recent fourth generation languages. In modern terms, high-level languages are not very powerful, but they are relatively easy to learn and use. They also have the advantage, in most cases, of being fairly standardized; indeed, the American National Standards Institute (ANSI) have specified a standard syntax for several well-known languages. Standardization is important, because it enables portable software to be written, which can transfer easily from one type of computer to another.

Most such languages rely on a *compiler* being available: a program which translates from the language to binary machine code. The original program is referred to as the *source code* and the binary code is referred to as the *compiled code* or the *object code*. However, some languages (such as BASIC) have an *interpreter* rather than a compiler; this translates the BASIC program as it is running, and does not produce an object version of the program. Software houses will normally only supply packaged software in the form of object code, which cannot be modified by users; source code presents too many opportunities to software pirates.

Figure 6.2 shows programs written in three well-known, high-level languages. Such languages are often classified as either *scientific* or *commercial*.

Scientific languages

Scientific languages include **FORTRAN**, **BASIC**, **PASCAL** and **C**. They are designed to perform complex calculations easily. They are also used for programming complex algorithms, where numerous alternatives need to be evaluated, in order to find the best solution to a problem.

FORTRAN (FORmula TRANslator) has been the most popular scientific language on mainframes since the early 1960s, and many of the commercially available packages for statistical analysis and engineering applications are written in FORTRAN. Much of this software has now been transferred down on to microcomputers, as good FORTRAN compilers have become available on micro-computers and as microcomputers have become powerful enough to

```
A similar section of program from the 3 languages for the
example cited in Question 1 and Figure 6.1.  The program
calculates the discounted sales value where discount is
given on all sales (at RATE1), but a higher discount (RATE2)
for sales of over 50 boxes.
[Note:  < denotes 'less than', > denotes 'greater than']

BASIC   200  LET SALES = PRICE*QUANTITY
        210  IF QUANTITY >= 50 THEN 240 ..ie go to line 240
        220  LET DISCOUNT = SALES*RATE1
        230  GOTO 250           .....ie go to line 250
        240  LET DISCOUNT = SALES*RATE2
        250  LET SALESVAL = SALES - DISCOUNT
        260  PRINT "DISCOUNTED SALES VALUE IS"; SALESVAL

COBOL   MULTIPLY PRICE BY QUANTITY GIVING SALES.
        IF QUANTITY IS LESS THAN 50
            THEN MULTIPLY SALES BY RATE1 GIVING DISCOUNT
            ELSE MULTIPLY SALES BY RATE2 GIVING DISCOUNT.
        SUBTRACT DISCOUNT FROM SALES GIVING SALESVAL.
        MOVE SALESVAL TO PRINT-VALUE.
        WRITE PRINT-LINE.

C       sales = price*quantity;
        if sales < 50 {
            discount = sales*rate1;
            }else{
            discount = sales*rate2;}
        salesval = sales - discount;
        printf("Discounted Sales Value is", salesval);
```

Figure 6.2   Typical statements from BASIC, COBOL and C

run mainframe software. FORTRAN is showing signs of becoming less popular for developing new software, but it will stay around for a long time, because so much current software is written in FORTRAN.

BASIC was developed originally for interactive use by students on mainframe computers. It is by far the most popular language on microcomputers, because it is supplied free with most home computers, and supplied as part of the Microsoft operating systems MSDOS and OS/2. It is probably the easiest language in which to write simple programs, and ideal for those who dabble in computing in order to get answers to mathematical problems. Much of the applications software on microcomputers is written in BASIC, because that was the only high-level language readily available on microcomputers when the software was developed. This is true even of commercial applications such as accounting.

131

BASIC is disliked by computer professionals because large programs written in BASIC tend to become very messy, which makes it difficult to update them or to find any obscure errors that occur in programs. The other major objection to BASIC is that it tends to be relatively unstandardized. Indeed, some manufacturers such as Data General have produced extremely powerful versions of BASIC which are quite different from other versions.

PASCAL developed in the 1970s, and is often used by colleges running Computer Science degrees, because it is not much more difficult to learn than BASIC, but is well structured as a language. Compilers are available on most computers from microcomputers to mainframes, and PASCAL is often used by scientists and engineers writing their own programs. PASCAL is also sometimes used for commercial software on microcomputers, but is probably little used for business software on larger computers.

C has only become popular in the 1980s; although it looks similar to PASCAL, it has been used mainly for packaged software rather than for writing applications programs. Many of the popular micro-computer packages have been rewritten in C, because it has the ease of programming of a high-level language, while maintaining much of the flexibility and efficiency of assembly code. C derived its rather strange name from its short-lived predecessors **BCPL** (British Computer Programming Language) and then **B**. C is associated with the operating system UNIX, and indeed much of UNIX is written in C. However, C compilers are becoming available on most computers and software houses are attracted to C because they expect software written in C to be far more portable than current versions of software.

Commercial languages

The only commercial high-level language in common use is **COBOL** (COmmon Business Orientated Language). Some older IBM main-frame software is written in PL/1, a language which was developed by IBM but no longer recommended by them. COBOL has been popular since the mid-1960s, and at least until recently, has been by far the most-used language for commercial applications on mini-computers and mainframes. Although versions of COBOL have been available, software houses have tended to prefer BASIC or PASCAL for writing commercial packages to run on microcomputers, for reasons already indicated.

One of the attractions of COBOL to software writers is that it has remained quite standardized, developing over the years as ANSI have regularly issued new standard specifications. As may be seen from the sample program in Figure 6.2, it is a wordy language and is intended to look like English. However, unlike English, you have to get the syntax exactly right if your program is to be understood!

The major advantage of COBOL is that programs have to be highly structured, and everything has to be precisely defined at the beginning of the program, including the structure of all files. Although it is quite impossible to write short COBOL programs, it does simplify all the statements concerned with updating files. Remember that commercial programs are concerned mainly with maintaining information systems and hence with updating files. It is for this reason that COBOL has usually been preferred for programming commercial applications.

Question

2 Bunthorne Ltd, a subsidiary of Conglomerate Plc, manufacture electrical equipment. Their sales ledger and stock control programs are written in COBOL, and they are commissioning your central computer department to write sales forecasting programs to analyse past sales and to extrapolate statistically.

   What would be the best language to use for these programs? How would you decide?

There is no clear answer to this question; one would need to know rather more before reaching a conclusion. COBOL might be the obvious language to use, since the current programs are written in COBOL. There would then be no problem about reading the files in from a COBOL format, whereas this might represent a problem in other languages. On the other hand, if complex statistical calculations are needed, then it would be very awkward to write the program in COBOL, and a language such as FORTRAN or BASIC might be preferable. Some other major points to be considered are:

● In what languages do your staff have substantial programming expertise?

- What programming languages do staff know at Bunthorne Ltd? It is preferable that they are able to understand the code, so that they can update the programs at a later date, if necessary
- For what languages are compilers available to Conglomerate Plc? No use recommending PASCAL, if this requires the purchase of an expensive compiler.

A large company such as Conglomerate Plc would normally standardize the use of a restricted set of computer programming languages. However, this would probably not help to answer question 2, as their standard list would normally include both a commercial language and a scientific language, the actual choice depending on the particular application.

Fourth generation languages (4GL)

Current computers are regarded as fourth generation computers, and some of the more recent languages which make powerful use of the facilities offered by this hardware, are therefore referred to as fourth generation languages, or 4GLs for short. Unfortunately, the term has been used in an extremely vague way by many software houses, who often describe their own packages as 4GLs in order to increase sales, without having very much concern for precise definitions.

The languages described so far are essentially *procedural* in nature: any program written in those languages has to be built up step by step. Fourth generation languages are designed to be 'user-friendly' and to require minimal programming effort; they achieve this by means of *non-procedural* elements, of which the following are typical:

- Data entry formats created 'on-screen', by means of a simple interactive process, the data entry routine then being called up whenever it is needed
- File structures defined interactively, and records entered and updated by means of single commands
- Report formats defined interactively, and called up by a program as required
- Single commands to call up selected records from a database, and print them according to a specified report format.

These save considerable effort, as most people find an interactive approach quite natural, whereas they find it difficult to write out a 'step-by-step' procedure correctly. In the same way, it is usually easier to draw a clear map to show someone how to reach your house (non-procedural) and more difficult to write out a clear and correct 'step-by-step' set of instructions (procedural approach). The earlier languages are concerned with *how* you achieve something, whereas current 4GL languages are concerned with *what* you are trying to achieve.

Programs written for commercial applications in a third generation language such as COBOL usually have a very large number of statements concerned with input, output and updating of files. A similar program written in a 4GL will therefore be much shorter, because these elements will be defined non-procedurally and will not have to be exactly spelled out. It is therefore not surprising that very high productivity gains are claimed for programming in 4GLs. It is usually estimated that it will take seven to ten times as long to develop a working program in a third generation language, as it will to develop the same program in a fourth generation language.

However, when it comes to a scientific program involving mainly complex calculations, most 4GLs will show far less productivity gains, and a language such as FORTRAN or PASCAL may well be preferable. This is because such programs are essentially procedural in nature.

Question

3 Which of the following are procedural, and which are non-procedural?
  (a) A recipe for cooking a fruit cake.
  (b) A map of your home town.
  (c) A workshop manual, showing how to replace defective parts of a motor car.

Regarding part (a), a recipe is normally a series of 'step-by-step' instructions, and is therefore procedural; indeed, a recipe is probably the closest analogy in everyday life to a computer program.

On the other hand, a map is essentially non-procedural, because it simply presents a picture from which you can work out your own route and your own instructions to get to the town hall, or to a friend's house.

A workshop manual is a good analogy to a program written in a 4GL, because it has both procedural and non-procedural elements. For example, you will find instructions in a workshop manual to remove an alternator, to strip it down part by part, and to reassemble it. However, most people would find such instructions impossible to follow on their own. The manual will therefore also include diagrams to make it clear, and these are non-procedural.

Development of programming expertise

Programming is a skilled art which requires an aptitude, and an ability to think logically. Even given the right aptitude, it still requires a significant amount of training and expertise before a trainee can become effective as a programmer. A trainee FORTRAN programmer will probably require a week's training course, plus a month or two before he really becomes effective. COBOL training can take twice as long, while assembly programming may require a six-to-nine month training schedule.

This represents a substantial investment by employers, as training courses now cost as much as £1000 per week, while a graduate trainee may cost £300 per week to employ when all overheads are taken into account. This probably means investing upwards of £3000 in a trainee programmer before he produces anything, and knowing that he may turn out not to have an aptitude for programming. Computer staff also tend to change jobs frequently, meaning that any investment by employers is likely to be lost. It is not surprising that many large companies are unwilling to take on trainee programmers, and smaller UK companies are notoriously unwilling to spend money on training.

One useful approach to developing software has been the use of *structured programming*, where programs are split into small modules, which can be tested thoroughly and eventually joined together. This has the advantage of allowing less experienced programmers to undertake the more straightforward modules, while more experienced staff program the difficult modules.

Even so, for many companies their investment in people is worth far more than their investment in hardware and software. There is no substitute for experience, and a good programmer with several years' experience may be ten times as productive as a mediocre programmer or a trainee.

136

Why use a 4GL?

The productivity gains to be derived from using a 4GL have already been mentioned i.e. that programs can be written seven to ten times as quickly using a 4GL instead of COBOL.

Another advantage of using a fourth generation language is that it makes it easier and therefore cheaper to train staff to write programs. The non-procedural elements of a 4GL tend to be very easy to learn, and a programmer only needs to learn how to program the procedural elements. Training courses are hence shorter, and it takes less time to get thoroughly to grips with the language.

A third advantage is that much of the programming work can be taken over by non-programmers, who find 4GLs very easy to use. An inexperienced user may find it easy to use a 4GL to read selected results from a database, and to print the results, but would never consider writing a program in COBOL to do the same. Thus, while there is still a need for skilled programmers when 4GLs are used, nevertheless much of the work previously undertaken by programmers can now be done by users.

The net effect is therefore to reduce drastically the cost of developing applications programs, and also to reduce the need for scarce, highly paid programmers.

Database packages

A database package is a package designed to create and update complex data files very easily. It should include these facilities:

- Defining record layouts
- Creating, amending and deleting records
- Indexing records by a specified field, or a combination of fields (e.g. customer code)
- Accessing individual records according to a specified index value (e.g. reading the customer record corresponding to a given customer code)
- Selecting all records which satisfy a specified condition (e.g. all employees aged under 40 with at least five years' service and earning over £400 per week)
- Sorting records into a specified sequence
- Defining report formats.

● Printing out data from selected records in the report format, specified and in a given sequence.

Fourth generation languages are often associated with database packages, to the extent that they are assumed to be the same thing. In fact, some simple database packages do not have command languages and some languages described as fourth generation are not primarily designed for manipulating databases. Nevertheless, most 4GLs are associated with database software, and we shall concentrate on such applications in the rest of this chapter.

There are many database packages with associated 4GLs available on minicomputers and mainframes; some run only on one operating system, or one make of computer, while others are available on several different computers. The best-known packages are probably Oracle, Ingres and Focus, but there are many others. Most of these packages have a Structured Query Language (SQL) interface, which is a standard set of commands for interrogating a database. This means that an SQL program should run equally well under Oracle, Ingres or any similar package. Printing out results requires the use of a non-standard report generator. Database packages usually also offer their own set of interrogation commands, which are more powerful and run faster than SQL but have the disadvantage of being non-standard.

Figure 6.3 shows some typical SQL commands.

Question

4 A sales/ledger invoicing system is being set up for a small wholesaler using a database package. List some of the database queries which would be most important to the wholesaler in controlling his business.

One could list an almost infinite number of queries, but we will concentrate on listing the questions that are of major interest to the business in maintaining good financial control. Some of the key facilities are:

● To view individual customer records and check them
● To view particular invoices as necessary

```
Insert into emp(name, pay, byear)        Update employee record for
   values ('Stang, Norman', 40000, 1953) Norman Stang, entering
                                          salary and birth year


copy table employee( ) into              Write the table to the
                'ourfile.dat'            file ourfile.dat


select   name, pay, dept, byear          Set up a table of selected
from     employee                        employee records showing
where    pay > 12500                     name, pay, dept and birth year
and      byear > 1950;                   for those born after 1950
                                         earning more than specified
```

Figure 6.3   Some SOL commands

● For a specified customer, to list the invoices outstanding and
  payments made against them, if any
● To have an aged debtors listing, showing amounts owed by
  customers, and the time periods for which the money is owing.

All of these are fairly standard database queries; the database would
need to contain at least two files. A customer file is needed for the main
customer data, but each customer may have several invoices recorded.
An invoice file is therefore also needed.

Disadvantages of database packages and 4GLs

One disadvantage of database packages, as compared with COBOL,
is the enormous load that they put on processors. When database
packages were first introduced in the 1970s, they were notorious for
slowing processors down to a standstill. With the more powerful
fourth generation computers now available, this is no longer such a
problem. However, it does mean that businesses will continue to use
COBOL or some other lower-level language for programs which are
frequently run and where speed is very important.

   As already mentioned, 4GLs are relatively unstandardized, and this
means that any staff recruited are likely to have to be retrained.
However, the major problem is the high cost of buying a 4GL; a 4GL
compiler is usually purchased as part of a database package, which
may cost as much as £100,000 on a large computer. Even so, many
large companies have invested heavily in 4GLs, because of the
enormous savings to be made on programming costs.

Using dBASE3 Plus: a practical case

dBASE3 Plus has been by far the most successful of the micro-computer database packages, and several million copies have been sold, if its predecessors (dBASE2 and dBASE3) are also included. As with many database packages, it can be operated by a series of single commands or by running a macro-program. A macro-program is simply a series of commands, and the commands are said to form a command language.

Some computer specialists would question whether the command language in dBASE3 Plus is truly a fourth generation language, because it lacks some of the advanced features that might be expected in a 4GL. Nevertheless, it has most of the features that we would expect from a 4GL and is well suited to illustrating the benefits of using a 4GL. dBASE3 also has the advantage of being relatively easy to understand, and is readily accessible on microcomputers to most college students. The example to be considered is a simplified sales ledger example, and is summarized in the following question.

Question

5 Baxter Clothes Ltd make clothes which they sell to retailers. They wish to set up a system using a microcomputer to keep a record of what they are owed by customers. The objectives of the system are:
   (a) To keep a record of all customers, together with the three amounts owing for the current month, for last month, and prior to last month, and the amount paid this month.
   (b) To allow records to be updated as appropriate.
   (c) To allow invoices to be entered against customer records.
   (d) To allow payments to be entered against customer records.
   (e) To print out details for customers of a specified size (small, medium or large).
   (f) To print out customers owing more than a specified amount, who have made no repayment so far this month.
   Design a system using dBASE3 to meet these objectives, and write a program or provide Baxter with menu-driven access to the system.

Many businesses have commissioned software to be written for them in dBASE3, because in this way they can commission bespoke software much more cheaply than with a conventional programming language. Microcomputer software tends to be relatively inflexible, whereas an applications program can be written to the precise specification of the user. We would expect many computer users in Conglomerate Plc to have information systems applications which justify writing bespoke software in a database language.

Writing software in dBASE3 is cheaper than conventional programming, but even so it is not cheap. A moderately complex application may well take ten to fifteen days' programming work; even doing the work 'in-house' is likely to cost well over £2000 when salaries and other staff overheads are taken into account. Where the work has to be contracted externally, consultants are likely to cost about £300 per day, so it would not be difficult to spend over £4000. On the other hand, even this expenditure may well be justified because of the savings to be made.

Regarding question 5, certain non-procedural steps are necessary to set the system up initially. The first stage is to define the file structure. The screen for defining the record layout is shown in Figure 6.4;

Bytes remaining: 3840

	Field name	Type	Width	Dec	Field name	Type	Width	Dec
1	CUSTNO	Character	8					
2	CUSTNAME	Character	20					
3	ADDRESS1	Character	25					
4	ADDRESS2	Character	25					
5	ADDRESS3	Character	25					
6	AMTOWE1	Numeric	9	2				
7	AMTOWE2	Numeric	9	2				
8	AMTOWE3	Numeric	9	2				
9	AMTTOTINV	Numeric	10	2				
10	AMTTOTPAID	Numeric	10	2				
11	BALANCE	Numeric	10	2				

CREATE | C: | LEDGER | FIELD 12/12

Enter the field name

Field names begin with a letter and may contain letters, digits and underscores

Figure 6.4 dBASE 3 screen for defining file layout

notice that companies are assumed to be classified by size as S, M or L (small, medium or large). The process of defining the record layout is initiated by the dBASE3 command:

Create ledger

This automatically sets up the sales ledger file LEDGER.DBF; as records will be referenced by the customer number, it will then need to be indexed by the command:

Index on custno to ledgerc

This creates an index file LEDGERC.NDX, which can be used to view the database records in customer number sequence, and to pick out individual records by customer number.

Finally the report layout needs to be specified, and this process is initiated by the command:

Create report ledger1

The report specification will be saved in the file LEDGER1. FRM, once it has been defined. The process of defining it is very easy, and is shown in Figure 6.5. It is simply a question of specifying the title of the report, and then defining for each field required: the column heading and the field width. Figure 6.5 shows the last field being entered on the screen; notice that dBASE3 shows the layout for the report, and one can easily go back to change this if it seems unsatisfactory.

We are now almost ready to run the system; it is only necessary to create a program file with a file extension of .PRG. This file can be created using a word processing package (in non–document mode) or using the editor in dBASE3. Assuming the program file is called BAXTER.PRG, then the command:

Do baxter

will cause the program to run. The actual program is shown in Figure 6.6, which also includes an explanation of what the various commands do. Notice that a necessary month-end routine is included, even though it was not mentioned in the original objectives. Figure 6.7 shows the opening screen display when the program is run; the user only has to type in the option required, in order to run that part of the system.

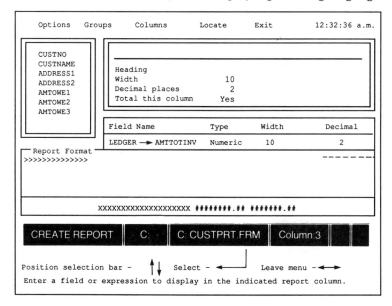

```
  Options    Groups    Columns      Locate      Exit      12:32:36 a.m.

┌───────────────┐  ┌────────────────────────────────────────────────────┐
│ CUSTNO        │  │                                                      │
│ CUSTNAME      │  │ Heading                                              │
│ ADDRESS1      │  │ Width                        10                      │
│ ADDRESS2      │  │ Decimal places                2                      │
│ AMTOWE1       │  │ Total this column           Yes                      │
│ AMTOWE2       │  └────────────────────────────────────────────────────┘
│ AMTOWE3       │  ┌────────────────────────────────────────────────────┐
│               │  │ Field Name          Type      Width      Decimal    │
└───────────────┘  │ LEDGER ──► AMTTOTINV  Numeric    10          2       │
┌ Report Format    │                                              ─ ─ ─ ─ ─│
│>>>>>>>>>>>>>>>    │                                                      │
│                  │                                                      │
│                  └────────────────────────────────────────────────────┘
│                  ┌────────────────────────────────────────────────────┐
│        XXXXXXXXXXXXXXXXXXXXX #######.## #######.##                      │
│                  └────────────────────────────────────────────────────┘
```

| CREATE REPORT | C: | C: CUSTPRT.FRM | Column:3 | |

```
Position selection bar -  ↑↓   Select -  ◄──┘    Leave menu - ◄──►
Enter a field or expression to display in the indicated report column.
```

Figure 6.5   dBASE 3 screen for dBASE 3 report layout

Expert systems

Since the early days of computers, there has been considerable interest in the idea of *artificial intelligence*, and especially of robots that could think for themselves. Considerable strides have been made in getting computers to think for themselves, but compared to human beings, computers are still pretty unimpressive in this respect. Computers have been taught to play chess up to good national standard, but it is unlikely that they will ever be able to compete with the top grand masters. The difficulty is that computers can assemble vast amounts of knowledge, and give the impression of thinking for themselves, but they cannot make the sort of leaps in thinking which defy logic and lead to important scientific discoveries.

Nevertheless, expert systems have been developed and found useful in certain situations. An expert system is a computer system which draws conclusions logically from a body of knowledge that has been assembled by that system. Thus, it is a computer program that would quite reasonably draw completely different sets of conclusions

143

```
*    client.prg  main program for Baxter Clothes Ltd
*              Sales Ledger System
*    Copyright Frank Blewett & Norman Stang, 1988
*    Programmer:  Frank Blewett  Version 30.9.88
clear
clear all
*             Put main menu on screen, and ask user to select
*
?'    -----Baxter Clothes Ltd Sales Ledger System-----'
?'    '
?'    1 - Update customer records'
?'    2 - Enter invoices'
?'    3 - Enter payments'
?'    4 - Print customer details by size'
?'    5 - Print debtor listing'
?'    M - Month end routine'
?'    Q - Quit'
*    Options 1-5 are objectives (b)-(f)
read
wait '  ' to choice
*                 now process option selected
docase choice
*                         OPTION 1  Update customer records
case choice = '1'
use ledger index custno
browse
*    Browse allows you to inspect the file, so as to amend or
*    delete records, and insert new records
*
*                         OPTION 2  Enter invoice amounts
case choice = '2'
use ledger index custno
clear
@1, 5 say 'Enter Invoice Amounts'
@3, 5 say 'Customer reference:' get custref
@5, 5 say 'Invoice amount:' get invamt
read
*    now find the record for that customer
find & custref
replace balance with balance + invamt
replace amttotinv with amttotinv + invamt
*    We have found the record for this customer, increased the
*    also adding to the total amount invoiced [amttotinv]
```

Figure 6.6   Macro-program for sales ledger system

```
*
*                          OPTION 3  Enter amount paid
case choice = '3'
use ledger index custno
clear
@1, 5 say 'Enter Amounts Paid'
@3, 5 say 'Customer reference:' get custref
@5, 5 say 'Amount paid:' get amtpaid
read
*now find the record for that customer
find & custref
replace balance with balance - amtpaid
replace amttotpaid with amttotpaid + amtpaid
*     Similar routine to Option 2, but decrease the balance
*     owing by the amount paid [amtpaid], and add to the total
*     amount paid [amttotpaid]
*
*                          OPTION 4  Print details by size
case choice = '4'
use ledger index custno
clear
@1, 5 say 'Print customer details'
@3, 5 say 'Customer size:' get custsize
read
report form custprt to print for size = custsize
*  print all records for specified size according to report
*                          format custprt
case choice = '5'
.....................
etc...................

Note: any lines of program which start with * are assumed to be
     comments in dBASE3
```

Figure 6.6—*contd.*

```
-----Baxter Clothes Ltd Sales Ledger System-----

        1 - Update customer records
        2 - Enter invoices
        3 - Enter payments
        4 - Print customer details by size
        5 - Print debtor listing
        M - Month end routine
        Q - Quit
```

Figure 6.7   Opening menu for sales ledger system

depending on what set of prior results had been fed to it. An expert system consists of 3 major components:

1   Knowledge base.
2   Logic: a set of 'if . . . then' rules to decide what conclusions can be reached about a particular case, using the knowledge base.
3   User interface.

Expert systems can be programmed in one of the standard high-level languages but it is better to use one of the languages specially designed for this purpose. There are several of these, but probably the best-known of these are PROLOG and LISP.

Probably the best-known application of expert systems has been in the area of medical diagnosis. It is often not easy to decide what is wrong with a patient from a whole series of symptoms, and doctors often would find it difficult to say why they reach particular conclusions. A number of attempts have been made to set up expert systems to cope with this task. While no substitute for an experienced doctor, such systems have been found to work reasonably well. They are likely to be useful in the training of medical students, and perhaps also in the diagnosis of relatively rare diseases.

Other promising areas are in the design of advanced manufacturing processes such as making electronic chips and in the diagnosis of faults in complex manufacturing equipment. Each of these requires knowledge and experience, in order to reach sensible conclusions.

Question

6   Let us return to you as Director of Management Information Systems at Conglomerate Plc. How do you decide what programming languages are appropriate for your company?

This question has not been explicitly answered by this chapter, but there have been good indications given. No one language can sensibly be chosen for all applications, but the following list covers most situations:

1   It is best to standardize on one scientific language (such as FORTRAN or BASIC) for writing programs to solve 'one-off' mathematical problems or forecasting and statistical applications.
2   COBOL is the obvious third generation language for commercial applications.

3   Small information systems are often best programmed by using a microcomputer database package such as dBASE3.
4   Where no suitable package is available, and a substantial amount of bespoke commercial software needs to be written, then it will be worth purchasing an appropriate 4GL.
5   Occasionally, specialist applications may require the use of assembly code or C or other languages. Similarly, specialist languages such as those used by expert systems may be appropriate in particular situations.

Most language compilers on mainframes and large minicomputers are relatively cheap or even free, and microcomputer software is also fairly cheap; the only major decision for the MIS manager, in this respect, is whether it is worth purchasing a 4GL. His other major problem, over a large company, is likely to be how to maintain a reasonable degree of standardization.

Assignment 6

An estate agent in your home town has asked you to set up a database of houses on their list to include: price, area, number of bedrooms, number of reception rooms and size of garden.

Set up a menu-driven system for them using dBASE3 (or any other suitable database package), which allows them to update the database and produce selected listings.

Recap

There is a wide range of programming languages, appropriate to different applications.
- The most common languages for *scientific applications* are FORTRAN, PASCAL and BASIC
- The standard third generation language for *commercial programs* is COBOL
- C is becoming increasingly popular for writing *packaged software*
- *Applications software* is now most commonly written in a *fourth generation language (4GL)* associated with a database package
- *Expert systems* are a means of programming computers to make decisions using special programming languages such as PROLOG and LISP.

Answers

1 See Figure 6.1
2 Either COBOL or a scientific language; each has advantages.
3 (a) Procedural.
  (b) Non-procedural.
  (c) Mixture of procedural (instructions) and non-procedural (illustrations).
4 (a) To view individual customer records and check them.
  (b) To view particular invoices as necessary.
  (c) For a specified customer, to list the invoices outstanding and payments made against them.
(d) Aged debtors listing.
5 See especially Figure 5.6; the accompanying text and Figures 5.4, 5.5, 5.7, and 5.8 are also relevant.
6 Scientific/statistical: language such as FORTRAN or BASIC
  Commercial: COBOL
  Small bespoke information systems: dBASE3 or similar
  Major commercial applications: a 4GL.

7: Applications software

Objectives

After reading this chapter, you should be able to:

- Describe the functions of the main accounting ledgers
- Outline the facilities offered by a microcomputer accounting package, and the advantages of using it
- Describe why adequate security and control are important in using accounting software, and how this can be established
- Outline the problems of implementing accounting systems on a computer
- Describe the range of software available, for other business applications.

Scenario

Imagine you are the financial director of a small company (Minnow Ltd), and are thinking about buying a computer for the first time. You need to decide which applications are worth running on the computer, and which packages to choose./What can a computer do to help you sort out the books? What benefits will you get from it? And what headaches could it give you? What other packages are worth buying, other than the standard accounting software?

Why use a computer for accounting?

Accounting is a key function in any business; if customers do not pay their bills, then the business cannot make money. Without a good accounting system, there is no way of ensuring that they do pay. Unfortunately, without a computer, accounting tends to involve rather a lot of tedious paperwork.

It is not surprising therefore that accounting has always been seen as one of the most obvious applications for a computer by large companies. More recently, accounting has been the most popular application for microcomputers by small businesses. There are three main advantages for a small business in using a computer:

1   Saving money by reducing staff costs.
2   Providing a more disciplined system, where information is immediately available.
3   Better management information.

Reduction of costs is the most obvious reason for using a computer, but in our experience, it is often not the major reason. Manual systems are all too often slightly chaotic, characterized by numerous bits of paper from which it is difficult to find out what is happening. Thus, the major motivation is often to get better information from a more reliable system. In this chapter, we shall concentrate on showing the type of management information reports that are available from accounting packages, but the other advantages of using a computer should not be ignored.

Integrated accounting packages

An integrated accounting package is one which can process all the standard accounting applications, and would normally include these modules:

1   Sales ledger.
2   Invoicing.
3   Stock control.
4   Purchase ledger.
5   Nominal ledger.
6   Payroll.

Figure 7.1 shows the interrelations between the various parts of the accounting system. In the next sections of this chapter, we shall consider the various modules in more detail.

There are numerous accounting packages on the market: for example, Sagesoft, Pegasus and Omicron on microcomputers; MSA and McCormack and Dodge software on larger computers. Most minicomputer manufacturers offer their own accounting software,

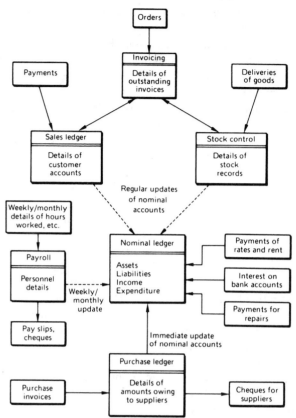

Figure 7.1   Integrated accounting system showing some of the more common transactions and how they are processed within a computer system

while some software houses offer packages which are available on several different computers.

Packages differ markedly in price (from £400 for Sagesoft to £100,000 or so for MSA on a mainframe computer). Not surprisingly, they also vary considerably in what they offer. Cheap microcomputer packages tend to be very inflexible in what they offer, and are designed specifically for the small business with very simple accounts.

151

For example, Sagesoft (at about £400) is a very popular accounting package at the cheap end of the microcomputer market, and is a 'user-friendly' package which many small businesses have bought 'off the shelf' and used without much difficulty and without any special training. Pegasus is probably the most popular microcomputer accounting package and costs about £1000 or so. It offers the more sophisticated facilities that one would expect from multi-user accounting software, together with a certain amount of flexibility in defining accounts and reports to be produced from the accounts. A company such as Minnow Ltd might well find either Sagesoft or Pegasus suitable for their needs. Further up the market, Omicron (at about £3000) and the various minicomputer and mainframe packages (£10,000 to £100,000) are designed to cope with complex multi-company accounting systems. The intention is to allow users enough flexibility to avoid having to tailor the package, or having to commission their own applications software. Software such as MSA includes many of the features of a database package, and in some respects is similar to using a 4GL for programming.

However, there is a trade-off in all software between flexibility and ease of use. The simplest packages to use are the ones which do a fairly simple job, and do not offer you lots of choices about what you do. As you have to make decisions, and think more about the best use of the software, it becomes more difficult to decide on a package. Where a package has complex programmable features, it takes longer to learn how to use, and a full training schedule for some of the larger mainframe packages can take as long as several weeks.

In the next sections of this chapter, we take a more detailed look at the purpose of the various accounting ledgers, and the information produced by a computer package. The package used for most of the sample outputs is the Pegasus Senior integrated accounting package. It obviously does not have the sophistication of the more expensive mainframe packages, but it is ideal to use in an introduction such as this and is a good, popular package.

Finally, remember that not all users bother to have an integrated accounting system. For many users, the major benefits are in sales ledger and invoicing, and they do not bother to put their nominal ledger and purchase ledger on to the computer. For this reason, most software houses also sell individual modules of their integrated accounting packages separately.

Sales ledger

The sales ledger (or account receivable) is the most important part of the accounts system for many businesses. It records for any customer what they currently owe, and the various transactions involving that customer. The main transactions are the recording of invoices and payments, but there may be others such as credit notes for returned goods. Figure 7.2 shows in more detail the processing that is needed.

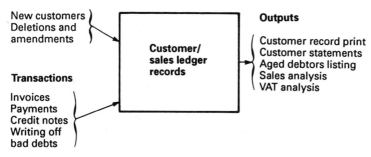

Changes to standing data

New customers
Deletions and
amendments

**Customer/
sales ledger
records**

Transactions

Invoices
Payments
Credit notes
Writing off
bad debts

Outputs

Customer record print
Customer statements
Aged debtors listing
Sales analysis
VAT analysis

Figure 7.2   Sales ledger processing

The first stage in setting up a sales ledger system is to create customer records, containing customer reference, name, address, contact name, discount rates allowed, and so on. The transactions can then be entered each day, and details of these will usually be kept within the database as a separate set of ledger records, indexed by customer reference so that the set of transactions for a specified customer can easily be retrieved.

The sales ledger is often run in conjunction with invoicing, and can then show significant cost savings. Run as a 'stand-alone' application, the cost saving is much less, but there are still advantages in terms of the better-quality information provided. The function of the sales ledger software is to maintain an accounting database, and this can be used to provide up-to-date and accurate information about any customer at any time. It can also be used to provide useful management information reports, about which customers are poor at paying their accounts. For example, Figure 7.3 shows one of the most

Students' Guide to Business Computing

useful reports, an aged debtors listing. Pegasus also offers various sales analysis reports, and a useful facility for printing out customer labels whenever you wish to mail them.

From the aged debtors report, you can see immediately the bad payers, who should be chased up by credit control staff. It also gives the senior management a good indicator of how the credit control system is performing. If the average time for customers to pay invoices is creeping up, then action needs to be taken. Otherwise, the company will be stuck with making interest-free loans to customers for longer than necessary.

[Courtesy of Pegasus Software Ltd]

SEA - SURE PRODUCTS (M-U) LTD.

23.06.89	Aged Debtors List			Page 1					
Account	3 Months	2 Months	1 Month	Current	Unallocated	Total	Cr Lim	Orders	Account Name
KER23154	125.45	915.57	557.00	876.23	97.21	2571.46	5000	0	Kerensa Nylons Ltd.
TAM00768	0.00	257.62	186.40	-0.63	212.56	655.95	5000	0	June B Tamsin Ltd.
WEN04435	17.30	-17.30	232.76	311.14	-183.00	360.90	25011	0 **	Wenna Steel Ltd.
	142.75	1155.89	976.16	1186.74	126.77	3588.31			

Figure 7.3 Pegasus: aged debtors listing

The problem for a small business is that there is always a need to pay suppliers and staff before receiving money from customers. This gap can only be covered by keeping a substantial amount of working capital in the business, and this probably entails borrowing money from the bank at a high rate of interest. At the worst, the bank may refuse to extend credit; small businesses often go bankrupt when quite profitable, because they run out of cash.

Even large businesses can have cash flow problems. If a large company over-extends its credit, then this can lead to loss of confidence by major shareholders and company directors may be forced to resign.

There is only one way of improving a poor cash flow position, and that is to maintain effective credit control by chasing up customers who are slow at paying. At the same time, you can reduce another headache for most businesses: bad debts. Unfortunately, all too many customers go into liquidation or disappear off the face of the earth. Make sure if possible that it is not your cash that disappears in the

154

process. If it does, then all you can do is to write the loss off in your accounts as bad debts.

Thus, computers can be a great help in providing your credit controllers with totally up-to-date information, on which customers to pursue, and precisely what invoices are outstanding from those customers.

The following question illustrated the cash flow problems involved in setting up a small business.

Question

1 Praxus Ltd are electrical wholesalers, who start business on January 1st with delivery of stocks valued at £500,000, which are replenished at the beginning of each month. They must pay their suppliers on the 25th of the month when the goods are delivered. Their sales to retailers during each month amount to £350,000 (for goods costing £250,000) and they are paid by retailers at the end of the month following, i.e. sales during January are paid for at the end of February. Praxus also have to pay rent, wages and administrative costs on the 21st of each month amounting to £60,000.

What is the maximum working capital required by the business, ignoring bank interest? If Praxus are paying 18% bank interest, what is the effective cost of this working capital?

Our approach to the question would be to list the payments and receipts for the first two or three months, when the major cash flow problems occur. We can list these in a table as below:

Date	Item	(Payment)/ Receipt	Net cash flow
21 Jan	Admin costs	(60,000)	(60,000)
25 Jan	Initial stock	(500,000)	(560,000)
21 Feb	Admin costs	(60,000)	(620,000)
25 Feb	Stock	(250,000)	(870,000)
28 Feb	Receipts	(350,000)	(520,000)
21 Mar	Admin costs	(60,000)	(580,000)
25 Mar	Stock	(250,000)	(830,000)
31 Mar	Receipts	350,000	(480,000)

Ignoring bank interest, Praxus Ltd is making a net profit of £40,000 per month, hence the cycle of payments will continue, but with the cash position improving by £40,000 each month. The maximum cash requirement is therefore £870,000; at 18% pa, or 1.5% per month, this would cost 1.5% of £870,000 = £13,050 per month or one third of the profit that Praxus Ltd are making.

Two points should be noted from this simple example:

1 Even fairly small businesses can have substantial capital requirements (the stock value for Praxus is relatively small).
2 Major savings can be made by good credit control. If Praxus persuaded their customers to pay a month earlier then this would reduce their working capital requirement by £350,000, making a saving of 1.5% of £350,000 = £5,250 per month.

Hence, effective credit control is extremely important.

Invoicing

Figure 7.4 shows a typical computerized invoice. For many businesses, order processing/invoicing is the application which shows the major cost savings, as well as providing significant benefits in other respects. In particular, many small businesses are involved in wholesaling or other similar distribution. For them, most of their administration is concerned with sales order processing. A typical business which is processing a hundred sales invoices per day, will probably have to process only ten purchase invoices per day.

Thus, the sheer volume of work on sales invoices suggests that it might be worth using a computer. There is also a significant burden of work in producing an individual invoice, which makes it a very good idea to use a computer. The reason is best illustrated by the following two questions:

Questions

2 What files and what data are needed in the accounting database, in order to produce an invoice such as in Figure 7.4? What input is then required to create the invoice?
3 Compare the process of creating a computerized invoice with the process of creating it manually.
    Explain why you would expect it to be easier to create the invoice, using a computer.

[Courtesy of Pegasus Software Ltd]

```
SEA-SURE PRODUCTS (M-U) LTD
Brikat House
35-41 Montagu Street
Kettering                          Invoice
Northants
Tel.(0536)522822             Number 40016
VAT Reg No 313 1976 17                 Date     Page
                                    01.06.89   1
```

```
Invoice to:            Deliver to:

Paul R Cox Ltd         Paul R Cox Ltd
15 High Street         Unit 2
Stevenage              Grange Industrial Estate
Herts                  Ripon
                       N Yorks
```

```
Despatched by: Data Post    Order No XXX9998      Account No COX88325
```

Qty	Description	Vat	Unit Cost	Disc	Total Cost
5	Sheet Metal 10/10	1	27.65	2.50	134.79
10	Auto Paint - Fern Green	1	1.13	3.00	10.96
10	Auto Paint - Merc Blue	1	2.04	5.00	19.38
15	Auto Paint - Delft Blue	1	1.82	3.00	26.48
20	Auto Paint - Fern Green	1	7.98	2.50	155.61

```
<-------- Vat Summary -------->
Code  %     Goods      Tax
1  15.00     329.86    49.48            Total Goods    347.22
                                        Total Vat       49.48
If paid within 7 or 30 days, you may deduct  Total Invoice  396.70
        17.36   or    8.68
from this invoice (respectively).
```

We should like to take this opportunity of thanking you for this order.
We hope we can be of service again at some point in the future.

Figure 7.4 Sample invoice

Regarding question 2, there are three main dimensions to the data accessed or updated, and hence three files would need to be accessed from the accounting database:

1 *Customer file* containing invoice address, delivery address, and referenced by customer account number. It will probably also contain summary details of the customer balance (i.e. how much they owe), which will be updated.

2 *Sales ledger file* which records details of individual invoices, and how much has been paid against those invoices. A new sales ledger record needs to be created each time an invoice is generated.

157

3 *Stock file* which includes product description, price, quantity in stock. The stock quantity will have to be updated for each item that is to be despatched.

Less obviously, there are certain system parameters which need to be accessed each time an invoice is created, and there is therefore a need for another small but crucial file:

4 *Sales parameter file* which contains various key accounting system details, such as latest invoice number, latest order number and VAT rates for different groups of products.

The input required to create the invoice is the customer account number and the stock reference number and quantity required for each of the stock items ordered. The remaining items on the printed invoice are either retrieved from files as described above, or are calculated by the computer program.

Regarding question 3, we have already described how an invoice is created on a computer system, although we did not fully describe the interactive process involved. For example, a good computer package will remind the operator if a customer is over his credit limit, and let the operator decide whether to proceed. If an item is out of stock, the computer will reject the item, probably offering the option of back-ordering it so that it can be delivered later.

Raising an invoice manually is a tedious business. Imagine yourself as a clerk sitting at a desk producing invoices manually. These are some of the steps involved:

1 Get out the customer record card and ledger card. Type invoice address and delivery address on to a blank invoice. Check that customer is not close to or over credit limit.

2 For each stock item ordered, get out the stock record card. Check that the quantity ordered is available, then update stock card and type product description, price, quantity ordered on to the invoice lines.

3 Calculate amounts for each item, and then invoice totals. Make sure that you give the appropriate discount in each case. Also calculate the VAT, remembering that certain items are not liable to VAT.

Thus, it is going to be much easier using a computer. This is particularly true when you remember that several order clerks are probably working together, each trying to access the same stock card at the same time. It is not surprising that many businesses see order processing and invoicing as the application where the highest benefits are to be derived from using a computer.

A major reservation is that somebody does have to enter all the data on to files in the first case. A relatively small business may have five thousand customers or more, and it takes substantial time and effort to enter those records, and then to keep them up-to-date. This is extremely worthwhile if the customers remain much the same, but the benefits will be less if a high proportion of customers is perpetually changing. Thus, there is little point in creating a customer record if you only sell to the customer once; you might just as well type the customer address direct on to an invoice.

Another problem is that many businesses are concerned with selling services, rather than goods. Businesses such as plumbers, photographers or management consultants will not issue line-by-line invoices such as in Figure 7.4. Instead, their invoice is likely to contain only one or two amounts referring to specific projects, with text explaining. Such companies will often not use invoicing software, and will only use a computer for sales ledger, if at all.

Question

4 Computer consultants very often do not use computers at all for their own accounting! Suggest reasons why this is so.

The obvious reason is a lack of faith in their own products, and there may be some truth in this! However, the major reason is that consultants tend to carry out relatively large projects for clients and therefore send out very few invoices (but for large amounts). This means that consultants often have very simple accounting systems, which are not worth putting on a computer.

Stock control

We have already mentioned in Chapter 2 (in relation to the burger bar) some of the problems associated with stock systems, and that a computer could be useful. Stock control software (sometimes referred to as *stock ledger* software) is perhaps more accurately described as stock recording software, since it provides a record of what is in stock rather than any elaborate control mechanism.

The objectives of a stock control system are as follows:

1 To keep an accurate record of what is currently in stock.
2 To minimize costs of buying and holding stock.
3 To minimize shrinkage costs.

A typical stock record print for the Pegasus stock control package is shown in Figure 7.5. A package such as this obviously meets the first objective, and provides the necessary database for the invoicing system that we have already discussed. The Pegasus stock record print not only includes the contents of the stock record, but also lists stock movements; details of these transactions are kept on a separate stock movements file.

Although it is a necessary basis for an invoicing system, some users see stock control as a useful 'stand-alone' application. It is quite common for small businesses to have hundreds of thousands of pounds tied up in stock, but not to know precisely what they have. With a computer system, you can print off a stock list at any time; manual systems tend to be haphazard, and sometimes no records are kept. Even if the records are accurate, producing a stock list would take far too long to be normally worth doing. It is also possible with a computer system to get summary prints of stock movements, so as to identify popular items. You can also highlight the 'slow-movers' i.e. stock items which gather dust on your shelves because they are totally obsolete; these can be scrapped, and space made available for more productive purposes.

Stock holding for any item is essentially cyclical; stock is delivered at the beginning of a cycle, and is then used up over several weeks or months; finally, a new batch of stock is delivered to replenish the stock and a new stock cycle begins. It is usually assumed that there are four main costs associated with stock control:

1 *Order cost* which is the cost associated with making an order, regardless of the size of order. The order cost includes the clerical cost in processing the order, together with any delivery charge from the supplier.
2 *Holding cost* which is a cost per unit of stock per day associated with

[Courtesy of Pegasus Software Ltd]

P23FERN12   /01   AUTO PAINT - FERN GREEN

Cost Code			Supplier Code	TUR04327
Stock Category	BS		Suppl Part No	190-SL1414-028
Factor			Supplier Code	
Assembly Indicator	N		Suppl Part No	
Unit Weight		0.00	Supplier Code	
Unit Volume		1.00	Suppl Part No	
Discount Code	A	40.00%	Alternate Ref	P1123/01
Discount Code	B	20.00%	Analysis Code	111S3
Discount Code	C	15.00%	Bin Location	P1
Qty Issued 1 Mth		283	VAT Code	1
Qty Issued 2 Mths		246	Cost Price	1.85/LITRE
Qty Issued 3+ Mths		873	Sell Price 1	3.95/LITRE
Last issued		25.02.88	Sell Price 2	3.80/LITRE
On order		450	Re-order level	150
Allocated		85	Re-order Qty	420
In stock		120	Minimum Stock	50
On Order		450	Re-order level	150
Allocated (Orders)		65	Re-order Qty	420
Allocated (B.O.M.)		0	Minimum Stock	50
Allocated (Manual)		15	Free Stock	35
In Stock		120		

Type	Date	Ref/order	Qty						
P/Order	11.02.88	PAD7532	10	Bal	400	Due 13.02.87	From TUR04327
Receipt	12.02.88	PAD7534	50				
S/Order	17.02.88	SED1321	150	Completed			
Issue	24.02.88	000001	45				

Figure 7.5   Stock record print

holding stock. It includes the cost of capital employed, and the warehousing cost.

3 *Stock-out cost* incurred when an item is needed and is out of stock. This may be an actual cost incurred by ordering at short notice at a higher price, or it may be an economic cost relating to loss of goodwill from customers who cannot be supplied, and may go elsewhere.

4 *Shrinkage cost* (already discussed in Chapter 2) is the cost of losing goods held in stock, due to deterioration or more usually due to theft by employees.

Questions

5 What is the relationship between order costs, holding costs and stock-out costs, and how can the total cost be minimized? How can a stock control package be useful in reducing these costs?

6 How can a stock control package be useful in reducing the level of shrinkage?

Regarding question 5, there is a well-known trade-off between order cost and stock-holding cost, described in most operational research textbooks. The obvious way to handle the problem of minimizing the total cost is to order a fixed quantity on each cycle when stocks reach an appropriate *reorder level*. But what is the right order quantity? A very small order quantity would ensure that average stock levels would be low and hence that the holding cost would be low, but at the expense of ordering frequently and drastically increasing total order costs. Conversely, low order costs can be achieved by ordering infrequently but ordering a much larger quantity; however, this means higher average stock levels, and hence much larger holding costs.

Clearly, the answer is to find an order quantity which leads neither to very high order costs nor to very high holding costs. It can be shown mathematically that minimizing the sum of the two costs does lead to such a quantity, by a formula known as the *economic order quantity*.

There is a similar, but more complex, trade-off between holding cost and stock-out cost. Stock-outs happen at the end of a stock cycle because things do not turn out as predicted: either demand is higher than expected, or a delivery is late. The net result is that even though a new order was sent in at the right time, the item is out of stock before the new delivery arrives. The way to avoid such stock-outs is to raise the reorder level to allow for possible variations. However, this does mean increasing average stock levels and hence holding costs in order to reduce stock-out costs. Again, the best balance has to be struck between two conflicting objectives, but here it is the correct reorder level that has to be selected.

Pegasus stock control software offers guidance in a fairly simple way regarding these two decisions: on the stock record (Figure 7.5), the user specifies a reorder quantity and a reorder level for each item. The reorder level is used to give warnings whenever the stock falls below that level, and to remind the user to reorder. The reorder quantity is offered to the user as the recommended quantity when they are issuing a purchase order. The reorder level and quantity can be calculated initially using estimated demand; they can then be reviewed regularly in the light of the actual demand shown in the stock issues report (see Figure 7.6).

Regarding question 6, the major fact or in reducing shrinkage is not the use of a computer, but good management. Some employees will steal if things are slack and they feel that they can get away with it; in parts of some companies, thieving seems to be regarded as a 'perk' of the job by certain employees. It is the job of management to ensure

[Courtesy of Pegasus Software Ltd]

SEA-SURE PRODUCTS (M-U) LTD

15.06.89	Issues Report (This Period To-Date)						Page 1
Stock Ref Location		Unit Desc	Qty Issued	Cost Value	Selling Value	Profit	Margin %
P1123 /01 Auto Paint - delft blue		L/TIN	107	176.55	456.89	280.34	61.36
P11MERC190 /02 Auto Paint - merc. blue		LITRE	926	1713.10	4290.40	2577.30	60.07
P12 /02 Auto Paint - fern green		S/TIN	732	753.96	1720.20	966.24	56.17
Total Issues			1765	2643.61	6467.49	3823.88	59.12

Figure 7.6   Stock issues report

that a strong system of controls is enforced, so that it is difficult to take things. If the management are concerned to enforce this, then the information provided by a computer system can be very useful. With a computer system, all stock issues have to be precisely entered, and it should be possible to identify where errors have occurred, if there are any problems. Most importantly, with a computer system, a selected stock list can be printed out as required; this makes it very easy to carry out random stock checks at any time, which are usually an effective deterrent against thieving.

Purchase ledger

At first sight, purchase ledger (or accounts payable) may seem similar to the sales ledger, except that it concerns suppliers rather than customers. In reality, the two are rather different; for example, there is no direct link between purchase ledger and stock control. The reason is that the stock quantities are updated by stock deliveries, which usually arrive a day or two before the corresponding purchase invoices.

A purchase ledger package can offer a number of useful facilities including the following:

1 Keeping track of what you owe your suppliers, and of how much has been paid against particular invoices.
2 Printing a list of invoices due for payment.
3 Printing remittance advices and cheques for any invoices selected for payment.
4 Printing a forecast of cash required for payments in the near future.

Figure 7.7 shows a suggested payment list produced by Pegasus; this, coupled with printing of remittance advice and cheques, is probably the most useful facility offered. The Pegasus purchase ledger package offers a number of other useful reports such as VAT analysis. It also offers an aged creditors report which is similar to the aged debtors report in Figure 7.4.

The purchase ledger is usually closely integrated with the nominal ledger, and it is normally the same staff who process both sets of accounts. The nominal ledger records the accounting data which forms the basis of the annual accounts, and a good computer system can substantially reduce the fees charged by your professional

[Courtesy of Pegasus Software Ltd]

SEA-SURE PRODUCTS (M-U) LTD

15.06.89		Suggested Payments List				Page 1
				Invoiced Amount	Discount Amount	Amount Due

FUR01224 Furndale Ltd

Reference	Date	Type	Discount			
INV5565	14.04.89	Invoice		143.75		143.75
INV01441	13.03.89	Invoice		79.99		79.99
INV92983	28.05.89	Invoice	3.00%	142.60	3.72	138.88
				366.34	3.72	362.62

HAR01110 Jones Transport Ltd   10 Days

Reference	Date	Type	Discount			
	01.03.89	Balance				134.00
	01.04.89	Balance				9.20
				0.00	0.00	143.20

Figure 7.7   Suggested payments list

accountant. It can also provide similar reports on a monthly or quarterly basis.

Question

7 What are the main components in the annual accounts? Why is it desirable to have such reports more than once a year?

The main components are:

1 *Assets*: what the business owns.
2 *Liabilities*: what the business owes (to shareholders, banks, creditors and others).
3 *Income*: what the business has earned over the period of the accounts.
4 *Expenses*: what the business has spent over the period of the accounts.

The first two components make up the *balance sheet* of the business, and give a breakdown of the valuation of the company at a specific date, namely the end of the period for which the accounts are produced. The second two components make up the *profit and loss account* for the period.

Statutory accounts are required annually for companies, but there are good reasons for producing them more often, for internal information. A lot can happen in twelve months, and it is important that the company gets an earlier warning of any possible problems. If costs jump or sales suddenly fall off, no sensible manager would want to wait for a year before taking action. It is therefore extremely useful to have accounts produced quarterly, and preferably monthly. If management accounts are needed frequently, then it becomes well worth while using a computer for the nominal ledger.

Nominal ledger

As shown in Figure 7.1, the nominal ledger (or general ledger) is the heart of an integrated accounting system. It contains the same items as the profit and loss account or balance sheet, but usually broken down into rather more subheadings. Each subheading is referred to as an account, and nominal accounts are designed on a double-entry basis, for example, paying a purchase invoice could invoice debiting the account for 'cash at bank' and crediting the purchases account.

For a small business, the nominal ledger may only contain about sixty accounts, covering major headings such as rent, rates, heating, wages, equipment, sales and various purchases. For larger businesses, the accounts will need to be split into cost centres (usually relating to departments), so that individual managers can be held responsible for their financial performance. This is normally done by comparing actual results with budgets agreed at the beginning of the accounting year. Figure 7.8 shows a typical monthly budget report produced by the Omicron nominal ledger package. The accounting variance shown is the difference between the actual amount and the budget in each case.

For a large company, the nominal ledger will be quite complex, and may include as many as ten thousand individual accounts. The software needs to be relatively sophisticated to produce reports efficiently. Accounts need to be accumulated in several different ways: for departments, for companies (where the main company has subsidiary companies), and to compare similar accounts across different sections of the company.

An upmarket microcomputer package such as Omicron is specifically designed to produce such reports from the nominal ledger, and even greater emphasis is placed on such reporting in the major mainframe packages. This reflects the fact that the major

[Courtesy of Omicron Ltd]

OMICRON POWERTRAINING
Actuals v Budgets for BRANCH A

For the current period ended 31/05/88

| CURRENT MONTH | | | | | YEAR-TO-DATE | | | |
ACTUAL	BUDGET	VARIANCE	VAR %	ACCOUNT DESCRIPTION	ACTUAL	BUDGET	VARIANCE	VAR %
44,566	53,250	(8,684)	(16)	Sales - Home	220,769	266,250	(45,481)	(17)
23,522	25,000	(1,478)	(6)	Sales - Overseas	126,193	125,000	1,193	1
0		0	0	Sundry Income	552		552	0
68,088	78,250	(10,162)	(13)	TOTAL REVENUE	347,515	391,250	(43,735)	(11)
28,544	25,000	(3,544)	(14)	Materials	152,510	125,000	(27,510)	(22)
28,550	27,000	(1,550)	(5)	Direct Labour	138,138	135,000	(3,138)	(2)
4,900	4,850	(50)	(1)	Salaries	23,588	24,250	662	3
5,350	5,350	0	0	Rent & Rates	26,000	26,000	0	0
400	350	(50)	(14)	Heat & Wages	2,467	1,750	(717)	(41)
232	232	0	0	Dep/n - Motors	1,160	1,160	0	0
425	425	0	0	Dep/n - Office Equip	2,125	2,125	0	0
825	825	0	0	Dep/n - P & M	4,125	4,125	0	0
198	325	127	39	Finance Costs	1,141	1,625	484	30
69,424	64,357	(5,067)	(8)	TOTAL EXPENDITURE	351,254	321,035	30,219	(9)
(1,336)	13,893	(15,229)	(110)	NET PROFIT/(LOSS)	(3,739)	70,215	(73,954)	(105)

Figure 7.8   Monthly budget report for a branch (Courtesy of Omicron Ltd)

accounting effort in large companies is concerned with internal budgeting and hence with the nominal ledger.

Payroll

Back in the 1950s when computers were first used in business, payroll was seen as the most obvious use for computers, and it is not difficult to see why. Payroll requires complex but routine calculations to deduct income tax (using the person's tax code and tax tables), pension contributions, national insurance payments, trade union subscriptions, and so on. It is obviously relatively easy for a computer to perform these calculations, and this will reduce costs, especially as most of the calculations are the same from week to week (or from month to month).

To use a payroll package, it is first necessary to define all the deductions specific to your organization; deductions such as income tax are obviously standard. The Pegasus payroll package allows up to 30 different special types of deduction to be defined; more expensive packages allow even more flexibility. Secondly, you need to define the records for individual employees, including name, date of birth, tax code, and salary; also specifying which deductions apply to that employee. Thirdly, you need to input for each pay period details of any overtime, expenses or other special payments for each employee.

A typical employee print produced by the Pegasus package is shown in Figure 7.9. As can be seen, there is not a great deal of effort in using such a package, and almost all large organizations use computers for payroll. Apart from producing the payslips, the computer package will also produce the credit transfer slips to direct the bank to pay the money into employee accounts. Another advantage is that various reports are automatically produced, which are needed by the Inland Revenue and the Department of Health and Social Security.

The only reservation about using a computer package is that it may not be worthwhile for a small business, because of the various complexities. The question of control may also be of concern to them, because payroll offers obvious opportunities for fraud. Thus, it may be better if they get their accountants or a computer dealer to process their payroll at a different location.

[Courtesy of Pegasus Software Ltd]

```
                     S-B Services Ltd

15.06.89          Employee Records              Page 9


P1JS012  Mr J Summerfield

Code        0033      SSP Days   1   Gross T.P.    259.45   Gross T.D.   7692.95
Tax Code    359H      Days/Week  5   Tax T.P.      125.00   Tax T.D.     1311.00
N.I. No.    PP123565N Sex        M   Net T.P.        9.63   Pens'n T.D.   123.12
Paid by     Giro                                           S.S.P. T.D.     9.35
C/Centre    PD02                     Average Pay   150.37
Birth Date  22.10.47  Hol Ent   20   S.S.P. Rate    9.3500
Start Date  12.01.75  Director   N
                                     <────────National Insurance────────>
Bank A/C    24566523 Co-operative Bank            'ERS    'EES    C/OUT
            20-45-80 Wellingborough   T.P. A       15.46   13.32

         Note:   T.P.= this period,  T.D. = year to date
```

Figure 7.9   Pegasus: employee print

Interrelations between the accounting ledgers

These are illustrated in Figure 7.1, and have already been referred to. In most accounting departments, it is usual for one group of staff to be responsible for invoicing/sales ledger and stock control, while a smaller group is responsible for nominal ledger and purchase ledger/payments. A third group would deal with payroll.

The updating of an integrated accounting system reflects this way of operating. Thus, there needs to be a 'real-time' link between order processing and both sales ledger and stock control, so that each time an invoice is created, the relevant sales ledger and stock records are updated.

The link between nominal and purchase ledger is also very important in a large organization, because purchases need to be charged against the correct nominal account, so that they are correctly included in cost centre accounting. The nominal ledger will also include accounts for different types of suppliers, and possibly even for individual major suppliers, so that these can be explicitly referred to in management accounting reports.

There is not the same need for a 'real-time' link between sales ledger and nominal ledger, and it is usually adequate to update the nominal ledger on a daily basis. Similarly, payroll does not need to be directly linked to the nominal ledger; it is enough to update the nominal ledger from the payroll system, each time the payroll has been run.

Contract accounting

Some accounting software (including most major mainframe packages) offers an additional facility known as contract accounting (or project accounting). This is similar to the nominal ledger, except the accounts relate to short-term projects, rather than cost centres. It is particularly relevant to contractors wishing to control project costs, and to consultants who need to present project accounts, because they charge clients on the basis of cost plus a fixed percentage. It is also important to certain other organizations; for example, the National Theatre expends large sums of money on new productions of plays, and it is important to ensure that these projects remain close to budget.

Question

8 Augustus Ltd sell a range of two hundred different gardening tools to two thousand retailers throughout the UK. Each retailer orders from them on average twice a month. Augustus Ltd have decided to implement a computer system for order processing and sales ledger.

 What problems are they likely to encounter? How long will it take them to implement the system?

Problems of introducing accounting software

Question 8 describes a situation similar to that of many first-time users of computers. There are four major problems that Augustus Ltd are likely to have to face:

1 *Selection of software* that meets their requirements. This is often difficult for a first-time user, because they may have no real concept of what a computer system can do.
2 *Installation of hardware*: for a multi-user system, this may take time to be delivered and to work effectively, particularly if a complex cabling network is necessary.

3 *Training of staff* needs to be carefully planned. This is likely to involve short training courses to familiarize staff with the accounting software, and to teach senior staff how to design suitable account coding systems. It will also take several days, if not weeks, of 'hands-on' experience for staff to become completely familiar and confident. Software houses usually provide sample data with their packages, to be used specifically for training purposes.

4 *File conversion*: the transferring of data from manual records to computer files. This is always the most time-consuming operation when implementing accounting software, and is discussed further below.

As indicated, the major problem for Augustus Ltd is file conversion. Suppose that it takes two minutes for each customer record that has to be entered initially; this is not a particularly generous estimate allowing for relatively inexperienced staff, and allowing for checking and corrections. This means that a total of four thousand minutes, or about three man-weeks, is needed just for entering the customer records. Even with three or four accounts staff sharing this work, it still represents a large task, particularly as some ledger details will also need to be entered. It is also necessary to enter the stock records, although this will be much quicker; two hundred stock records, at two minutes each, would take only a total of one or two man-days.

The major problem with file conversion is that the accounts system still has to keep running while the change-over is happening. Moreover, the same staff have to keep the old system running while introducing the new computer system; the difficulties of managing the changeover are discussed further in Chapter 8. The only way to manage this is to progress in small steps; for example, Augustus could start by entering one group of customers on to the computer, and could get the accounts system working just with that group of customers. They would then enter a second group, and implement the computer system for them; and so on, until all their customers are 'live' on the computer system. Once the sales ledger is operational, they can then start implementing the other accounting ledgers, if that is the plan.

In other words, successful implementation can only be achieved by a carefully phased schedule, which would normally be drawn up by Augustus Ltd and the dealer from which they buy the accounting software, who would be able to advise them on likely problems. Even so, implementing the system is likely to involve months of stress and overtime for their accounting staff. The only satisfaction is that it is probably the only time that it needs to be done. With any luck, when Augustus decide to upgrade their computer in three or four years' time, they should be able to transfer their accounting data to the new computer without needing to type it . . . but even this is not guaranteed!

Problems of security and control

A high degree of care is essential with any accounts system, and potential users of computers are often worried whether their accounting data is really safe on a computer, since a badly managed system could easily bankrupt their business. In fact, a well-managed computer system should be far more reliable than a manual system.

The following objectives need to be considered carefully, for a computer-based accounts system:

1   To prevent fraud.
2   To prevent errors occurring and thus ensure that the accounts are correct.
3   To maintain confidentiality where necessary.
4   To protect the accounting system against computer malfunctions, and against natural hazards such as fire and floods.

Confidentiality is necessary to prevent competitors getting vital sales information from you about which products are selling well or badly. Even your customer list may be valuable to your more dubious competitors. It is also important to keep confidential any information about what your customers owe you, if you wish to maintan a friendly relationship with them.

The other need for confidentiality is in relation to individuals, usually where data is held for payroll and personnel reasons. People often do not wish to have their age or salaries revealed and, in any case, this is subject to the 1985 Data Protection Act in the UK. This act specifies that any holder of such data on a computer must register; that they must take adequate steps to ensure that the data is accurate and kept confidential; and that individuals have the right to see their own record, on request, at a nominal fee.

It is never possible to establish absolute security, and even top

American defence computer systems have been successfully breached by outside coding experts who were invited to test the systems. Apparently secure commercial systems can be intercepted by experts using 'bugging' equipment to pick up radio-wave emissions from computer cables. Nevertheless, there are certain simple rules which can establish a system which is adequate for most situations.

Multi-user systems

Most accounting work is processed on multi-user systems. Strong control is needed because where mistakes (or even fraud) occur, you have to be able to identify the person responsible. This can be easily achieved, by a system of accounts and passwords, where each person using the system has to give an *account number* and *password* to log in to the computer. Usually, further passwords have to be given to reach particular parts of the software; for example, a sales clerk might be allowed access to the sales ledger but not to the nominal ledger. Some operating systems allow the level of access to be defined for each user; thus, a senior manager requiring information may be permitted only to read data files, while other users are allowed to update the files.

Such a system requires a *controller* to monitor the system, usually a senior member of the accounts staff. Their job is to create accounts for staff on the system, and to allocate passwords, and to change the passwords at regular intervals. This is mainly to encourage staff to be strict, but it also deters hackers where the computer has an outside telephone link. Most hackers get into computer systems not by doing anything clever, but by using popular passwords such as GOD, FRED, BOSS and PASS; other hackers get into systems because ex-employees pass on lists of passwords, which are still unchanged after a year or two. Some users even help hackers by fixing a piece of paper to their computer terminal with their password written on it.

Apart from using passwords, the other crucial facility is that the software maintains a good *audit trail*. This is a log of all transactions entered into the accounts system, and kept on a disk file which can be printed out once or twice a week. All transactions are recorded against a user account number, and the audit trail can only be accessed by the controller of the accounts system. This means that fraudulent activity can be traced back to the account responsible; similarly, any rash of errors in the accounts system can probably be traced back to a new, incompetent employee. The audit trail also tells you exactly what has been entered; this means that you can not only identify errors, but you can also correct them.

In summary, a system such as described can protect your accounts system from criminals, hackers and incompetent employees. However, it still requires determined management. If passwords are left unchanged, if staff are allowed to borrow one another's accounts, and if the manager never bothers to check up, then a poor accounting system will develop.

Single-user systems

These are used at the most by two or three staff (at different times) and should present less control problems where used for accounting, because the scope for fraud by employees is obviously much less. If the employer wants to defraud himself, presumably no accounting system is going to prevent him. Nevertheless, it is worth having passwords, to prevent unauthorized users from accessing the system. An audit trail is also essential, in order to be able to identify and correct any errors made.

However, the worrying thing about microcomputers is the total lack of security shown by many users. A microcomputer with a hard disk can hold most of the financial data that is worth knowing about a large company. This is often immediately accessible to any stranger with a copy of Lotus 1-2-3 and Wordstar, who wanders into the office when it is empty. Sometimes, the user will thoughtfully leave software on open access as well. In a few moments, the stranger can copy any data files and confidential memos that they want, and then wander out, leaving the user totally unaware that anything has happened. Alternatively, they can use the opportunity completely to wreck many of the data files on the hard disk.

The only total protection against such activity is to lock the computer disk unit in a safe when it is not in use. A lower level of protection is provided by the keyboard lock on many microcomputers . . . but how many users even use such locks when they are provided? Probably the best solution where security is important is to use a package such as Fortress Plus from Deloitte Haskins.

Fortress Plus is a program which runs in conjunction with a special 'add-on' board; this ensures that you can only log into the computer if you give an acceptable password.

Other features offered by Fortress Plus include:

- The microcomputer is automatically logged off if it is left unused for more than a specified time
- Facility to code and decode files, using complex algorithms based on your own coding keys, and making it almost impossible for someone else to make sense of your files
- Total deletion of files by writing zeroes over the entire disk area occupied by the file.

The last facility is extremely important. Many users do not realize that a DELETE command in most operating systems does not actually delete the file; it merely removes the name from the directory. It takes only a few seconds to restore accidentally deleted files using a package such as the Norton Utilities. Equally, it is easy for an unscrupulous outsider to restore files for some devious purpose, that you thought were deleted.

Question

9 Berners Paints Ltd use a computer for accounting, which has been destroyed by a serious fire. What costs will they incur in restoring their computer system to its previous level, if no precautions had been taken? What precautions should Berners have taken beforehand, to ensure that their accounts system is not seriously affected by this disaster?

Fires, floods and other disasters

If you think back to Chapter 5, it should give you some ideas regarding this question. The likely problems that Berners will face are:

1 *Hardware*: they will need to buy a new computer. This should not be a major problem, unless their computer is fairly large. In any case, it should be possible to buy time on other computers in the short term.
2 *Software*: packaged software should be easy to replace, at a price. Bespoke software may be difficult to replace.
3 *Data files*: this represents the major investment. If these are lost, the whole accounts system and hence the company could be lost. Even

if the accounts files could be restored from computer printouts, this could take several man-months of effort.

Thus, hardware and packaged software should not represent a major problem for Berners Ltd; it should be possible to restore these fairly rapidly, and presumably the cost will be paid by the insurance company. The major problem would be in restoring any bespoke software, and the accounts data files.

As the question indicates, the answer is to take precautions beforehand, by taking 'back-up' copies and keeping these at another location. Copies of software should be taken whenever changes are made to the software. The data files should be backed up regularly (probably daily) on to a disk or preferably to a tape cassette using a fast back-up device. The 'back-up' copy can be kept at another office, or even at the manager's home, for a small business. In the event of a fire or flood, the 'back-up' files can be copied on to the hard disk, and the accounts system restored rapidly. Indeed, it is not unknown for accounts systems to be back in operation within twenty-four hours of such a disaster.

A more common problem is that of computers malfunctioning. It is possible for computer files to become corrupted when this happens, particularly when a hard disk goes wrong. Again, the solution is to keep taking 'back-up' copies, to ensure that nothing significant is lost when it does go wrong.

Useful standard packages

There is an enormous number of packages on the UK market, some of general interest, others aimed at very specialist areas. In the remainder of this chapter, we aim merely to give a brief indication of what is available for applications other than accounting.

Word processing

WP is probably the most popular application for microcomputers, and in many large companies, a word processor is considered as necessary as carpeting and expensive furniture. It is also genuinely very useful in many situations. The facilities offered by WP include:

● Documents are typed directly on to a screen, and can easily be corrected by inserting and deleting text, or over-typing

● Document margins can be changed at any time, and a section of the text reformed to fit within the new margins
● Text substitution can be made automatically e.g. replacing 'microcomputer' by 'micro' throughout the document
● Blocks of text may be moved or copied from one part of the document to another
● The completed document may be saved to a disk file, and retrieved later for further editing
● While editing a document, other document files may be inserted at any point
● The disk file may be printed out at any time
● Personalized letters may be produced for mailing, by typing a standard letter and using a file of names and addresses.

A good microcomputer set-up for word processing is much more expensive than an electric typewriter, but the cost can be justified in many situations. Word processing is extremely useful where long reports have to be produced, which require careful drafting and several stages of re-editing. For example, this book has been typed using Wordstar, saving considerable effort in sticking and pasting.

Word processing is also extremely useful for a solicitor or a surveyor, where contracts or specifications have to be typed which include many standard clauses. Finally, it is invaluable where numerous standard but personally addressed letters have to be sent out for mailing purposes.

For a fuller description of word processing, see reference 1.

Electronic mailing

Electronic mail is well established as a means of fast and relatively cheap external communication, via Telecom Gold and other such networks. Increasingly, many large companies are seeing similar internal communications as necessary, although it often represents an expensive luxury. Electronic mail can be run on a microcomputer network, but to be really effective requires a large minicomputer with a package such as the Wang Office Systems software to control operations.

Electronic mail requires a microcomputer or terminal in every department, with access to word processing software, necessary to produce the document in electronic form. The advantage is that where a memo needs to be sent to all staff, or to a selected group of staff, then this can be done instantly. In theory, this is a 'paperless' transaction because the receiver can just read the message off the screen. In practice, the message will almost certainly be printed off by the receiver, unless it is very short.

Often electronic office software also includes electronic diary software, to enable staff to enter their appointments. Theoretically, this enables staff to book meetings easily, where several other staff are involved, and such systems have been used very sucesssfully by senior civil servants booking appointments for government ministers. However, in most organizations, electronic diaries have proved a dismal failure. This is partly because of human laziness in not entering their appointments and partly because of the 'twit' factor i.e. senior managers will not use a system where 'some twit that I am trying to avoid can ring up the computer and make an appointment with me'.

The major problem with electronic office systems, apart from the cost of the networks and the software, is the central processing power required. The software needs to be permanently running, so that it can immediately transmit any messages sent by users; also, if the system is successful, it will generate a lot of extra use of the computer. The net effect is that organizations which install office systems very often find before long that they need a second processor to support it.

Financial planning

This is an important area for all businesses. Sensible planning for several months or years ahead allows management to forecast their cash needs, so that they can arrange bank loans or cut back slightly if necessary.

The most popular software for financial planning are spreadsheet packages such as Lotus 1-2-3 and Supercalc. A spreadsheet simply gives the user a blank table into which they can enter text, data or formulae. The rows represent variables such as price and quantity sold, while the columns represent time periods. Most formulae in a financial planning model are fairly simple, such as:

Revenue = Price * Quantity sold

The advantage of using a computer model is that you can easily re-calculate your results with a new set of data. Thus, you do not have to look only at one scenario, but can see what happens if sales are better or worse than expected.

Spreadsheets are also very useful for many situations other than financial planning and can be used whenever it is necessary to perform some simple calculations, and then print out a result. For a fuller description, see reference 2.

More complex modelling problems may require financial modelling software, where a separate logic file is set up instead of including formulae in the spreadsheet table. Probably the best-known package in the UK on mainframes and minicomputers is FCS-EPS, which has a micro version known as Micro-FCS.

Graphics

Most spreadsheet packages have good, basic facilities for printing graphs, bar charts and so on, which are useful for illustrating business reports. More specialist packages such as Microsoft Chart offer far more flexibility in the types of graph that can be produced, and in designing the layout of the graph.

Further upmarket, there are a number of packages, designed to produce business graphics in very high-quality colour output. The output can be via a graph plotter onto paper or overhead projector slides, or special devices can be used which produce 35mm slides. One such package is Harvard Presentation Graphics, available on microcomputers. However, the best packages are undoubtedly SAS Graphics and ISSCO Graphics, which run on large minicomputers and mainframes. These include maps, three-dimensional graphs, and many other features, and are not cheap; ISSCO sells for over £20,000.

Another fast-growing area is the use of computers for computer-aided design (CAD) by designers, draughtsmen and architects. The best systems use graphics workstations with specialist software. However, there is a number of good packages available on microcomputers such as Autocad and Robocad; these now include libraries of symbols designed for specific users such as architects. Use of these packages is proving a quicker way of producing architects' drawings, and is particularly good where drawings need to be re-done several times.

Desktop publishing

This is a development which has only been made possible by the introduction of cheap laser printers. Essentially, a DTP package has most of the facilities of professional typesetting equipment at a fraction of the price. The facilities offered by DTP include the following:

- To type and edit text
- To modify text to any required character size and font
- To import text files produced by any popular word-processing package
- To import graphics files produced by any popular spreadsheet or CAD package
- To manipulate text (by re-forming it within new margins) and graphics (by expanding or shrinking it), in order to be able to achieve a suitable design layout.

Desk top publishing software is extremely useful for anyone in a business needing to produce a regular newsletter, either to inform customers of new developments or for internal circulation. It is used normally to set up the final layout, with the text being imported from a word-processing package, any tables being imported from a spreadsheet, and pictures from a graphics package.

Other applications

Any part of an organization which is involved in analysing data is likely to be able to justify using at least a cheap microcomputer, and that applies to most areas of business. In this section, we look at the software available in three areas, but there are others that could be considered.

Personnel and manpower planning
A good personnel records system is essential to any large organization, in order to provide the right information to management in making decisions, such as:

1 *Wage negotiations.* The trade union proposes that a 'loyalty' bonus be paid to all electricians with over three years' service. How much will this cost the company?
2 *Internal promotions.* What staff should be considered for a particular appointment, given that they need to have certain skills and experience, and they would need currently to be at a lower salary?
3 *General reviews of staffing problems.* What are the staff like, from the point of view of age and experience? To give an effective answer

requires breakdown of staff of different skills by age and length of service, and probably also selected listings.

4 *Manpower planning.* What staff need to be recruited at different levels, in order to ensure that we have the right number of skilled staff in five years' time?

This is a very obvious application for a database package, where staff data is appropriately classified. It needs to be closely integrated with the company payroll system, so that then the personnel records can be automatically updated with very little effort. This also ensures that the personnel records will be up-to-date, because no employee will tolerate inaccuracies in their pay for long.

A manpower planning system could be implemented using a standard package such as dBASE3 Plus, but there is a number of packages available specifically designed for this purpose, which are much easier to use. It also saves 're-inventing the wheel', because the problems faced by a personnel department have probably already been solved by previous users of manpower planning software.

Marketing and market research

Marketing is concerned with planning how to sell products; market research is concerned with investigating whether there is a market for new products, and whether current marketing is effective, by means of interviews and questionnaires, and by analysis of sales. Obviously, the two functions are closely linked, and are usually part of the same department.

Extremely useful sales analysis is provided by any good invoicing software. For example, it can tell you the monthly sales of each product, and how well different groups of products are selling to various types of customer in various parts of the country.

Marketing departments often make use of computers for 'one-off' analysis, using spreadsheets or short programs written specially for the task. Specific applications involving use of packaged software include:

1 *Survey analysis.* One well-known package is SPSS, but there are others. Such packages include cross-tabulations of results, and a wide range of statistical features.

2 *Sales forecasting.* Sophisticated statistical methods have been developed for forecasting, and there are numerous packages which

include such facilities. Marketing specialists have also developed a number of packages which use advanced modelling methods to predict the effect of advertising and other factors on consumer sales.

3   *New product development.* In assessing the viability of a new product a short-to-medium term financial plan is usually needed. This is an obvious application for a spreadsheet or financial modelling software.

Production planning

Production scheduling and planning is a complex area, requiring optimal planning to raw material stocks and finished goods stocks. You also need to make sure that machinery is used close to 100% of the time, by efficient scheduling. This is not at all easy where different-sized items are produced on the same equipment, requiring a new set-up for each new batch.

Many packages are available for production and stock recording, and even this can be very useful, with a complex multi-stage production system. More sophisticated software will produce production schedules, and this usually includes an interactive module, so that the user can modify the schedules, if they do not quite fit what is needed.

Specialist applications

To illustrate the sort of specialist software that is on offer, we consider the facilities in packages aimed at three specific operations:

1   *Insurance agents.* Software can automatically print reminder letters to clients when premium instalments or renewals are due. It can provide an accounting system, and ensure that insurance companies are paid on time. Selected clients can easily be mailed for promotional purposes.

2   *Football clubs.* Apart from the standard accounting and mailing-list applications, many professional football clubs are now using computers for ticket booking. This reduces the administrative effort, because seats can be automatically reserved each week for season ticket holders, or blocked off for visiting supporters. It also enables tickets to be sold from terminals in several different offices, without any danger of double-booking.

3   *Transport hauliers.* Fleet monitoring software is available which uses tachograph output to produce necessary reports, and to monitor the operational efficiency of the lorry fleet. Many large hauliers also use vehicle scheduling software to produce daily routeing schedules.

Whatever type of business you wish to consider, there is certain to be microcomputer software designed for its needs. We know of successful packages for doctors, dentists, estate agents, farmers, pubs, garages and many others.

Assignment 7

(a) Choose a local small business known to you that uses a computer for accounting. Find out what the original schedule for implementation was, and how long it actually took, and what problems were encountered. If they did the implementation in stages, find out how many records needed to be entered at each stage.

   Write up your report as a case history, explaining also what benefits the company feel that they have got from using a computer for accounting.

(b) Choose a large Public Limited Company (PLC), and find out as much as you can about their range of commercial activities. Identify as many application areas as possible, where a computer could be useful, and explain in each case why it would be beneficial.

Recap

The most important computer application for most businesses is **accounting**, and especially *sales ledger* and *invoicing*. Other applications included in integrated accounting software are: *stock control, purchase ledger, nominal ledger,* and *payroll*.

The benefits of using a computer for accounting are *reduced costs*, a *more disciplined system*, and *better management information*.

The major problem associated with an **accounts system** is the amount of time and effort needed in **implementation**, in order to train staff and complete the process of file conversion.

Security and control is of key importance with an accounting system. It is essential to establish a system of passwords and a good audit trail. A regular system of *backups* and storing of back-up files at another location is essential, in case of files getting corrupted and also to be able to re-establish the system in case of fire or flood.

Standard software useful to many businesses include *word processing (WP), electronic mail, spreadsheets, graphics* and *desk top publishing (DTP)*.

Application areas where computers are used include *Personnel and Manpower Planning, Marketing and Market Research*, and *Production Planning*.

Specialist software is available for most operations, including insurance agents, professional football clubs, transport hauliers, and many others.

Answers

1 Maximum £870,000; equivalent to cost of £13,050 per month
2 Files: customer file, sales ledger file, stock file, sales parameter file.
 Input: customer account no, stock ref.no(s), quantity ordered
3 Easier to use a computer because you do not need to get information from various ledger cards, and update the cards; instead, the data is immediately available and updated by the computer, and the invoice is automatically printed.
4 Because their accounts systems tend to be very simple, with relatively few invoices.
5 Order costs reduce as orders increase in size; stock-holding costs increase as orders increase. Hence, there is a trade-off to find the optimum order quantity.
 Similarly, there is a trade-off between holding costs and stock-out costs to determine the optimum safety stock.
6 A good computer package can provide the information to enable management to establish good control, especially by doing regular stock checks.
7 Assets, liabilities, income and expenditure. A lot can go wrong in a year, and quarterly or even monthly reports are therefore highly desirable.
8 Selection of software; installation of hardware; training of staff; file conversion.
 Schedule for implementation essential; likely to extend over several months.
9 Replacing hardware; replacing software; restoring data files. The major precaution is to keep back-ups of data files, and possibly software.

8: Systems testing and implementation

Objectives

After reading this chapter, you should be able to:
- Explain the methods adopted for testing
- Describe the value of prototyping and the use of 4GL systems
- Explain the importance of the training of users
- Outline the various methods of changing over from the old system to the new
- Describe how systems development is managed.

Scenario

Imagine you are a systems analyst in a fairly small company which has decided to computerize its payroll system. You have done the necessary analysis and logical design. In this you have followed the guidelines given in earlier chapters. You have also written detailed specifications to enable the company's programmer to write the required programs.

Program and systems testing

We will assume that the programmer has written the programs according to your specifications. How do you know that the programs work? Clearly you will have to test them.

Questions

1 List the various forms of testing of the payroll that you would expect to be undertaken.
2 What are the main sources of test data?

In preparing a list in answer to question 1, we categorized testing as follows:

1   *Program testing*. This is undertaken by the programmer. This is to test the program to ensure that it rejects invalid data, performs its calculations correctly on valid data, and produces output in the desired format. The programmer will normally prepare test data to do this, and programs are tested as individual units.

Even the testing of individual programs can take a number of forms. First, the programmer might *desk check* the program. This entails sitting at the desk and taking an input transaction right through the series of instructions as written, making a note of changes in the values of the variables. In this way, by using pencil and paper, the programmer simulates the computer's actions.

Secondly, the programmer will have the program compiled and will remove any syntax and compilation errors. Syntax errors are grammatical mistakes such as omitting compulsory full stops or incorrectly constructing statements. Compilation errors are those which can arise through mis-spellings or other mistakes in the entry of the source program. Test data can be fed through the program and the results checked. Any unexpected results will result in amendments being made to the program. Some systems allow for programs to be interpreted until the program is in its finished state. Only then will it be compiled and linked into the system. (Chapter 6 explains the differences between interpreting and compiling.)

Thirdly, in structured systems each program is written as a series of self-contained modules. The programmer will engage in *bottom-up testing*. Here a specially written small *driver program* will control the testing of each module separately. This technique is especially useful for large programs which might be written by two or more programmers.

2   *Top-down testing* is also associated with structured systems. Here the purpose is to ensure that the hierarchical structure of the program calls, works correctly. A structured system often works on a hierarchy of menus. It is important to ensure that the user is able to work down the series of menus to request a specific program. It is equally important to ensure that after the program has been executed, control returns to the appropriate menu.

3   *Systems testing*. This could be described as *testing of integration*. This

is normally directed by the systems analyst. Its purpose is to ensure that the individual programs link together properly. This means that where program A is intended to use as an input, the output from program B, it can actually do so.

4 *Timing testing.* This is a system test designed to see that the system process transactions within the expected period of time. It might examine the time taken to respond to a query. It is important to ensure that such tests are conducted under realistic conditions.

   This form of testing is particularly important for a time-critical system like payroll. Staff must be paid on time and you have to meet the bank's schedules.

5 *Peak load testing.* This is to ensure that the system can handle the maximum number of expected transactions within a given time period. This is often linked to timing tests. For a one-off application such as payroll you will need to test the effects of having other applications using the computer simultaneously. You may find it necessary to have other jobs rescheduled.

   In general terms, peak load testing is important. This is evidenced by the failures of the London Stock Exchange system to cope with the initial flood of data accesses.

6 *Back-up and recovery testing.* This is a test of the procedures relating to backing-up the system in the event of a breakdown. A breakdown is simulated and then the system re-started. The test is designed to see whether all the transactions prior to the breakdown are saved.

7 *Human procedure testing.* Not only is it important to test the computer procedures; it is also necessary to ensure that people responsible for data entry perform their jobs correctly. This would include seeing that users follow correct log-in procedures, and that they log-off when they finish, rather than leave the VDU switched on and available to possibly unauthorized users. Similarly, you would want to see what users do if the computer does not respond to their enquiry immediately. For a sensitive system such as payroll, testing for security against unauthorized access is particularly important.

To answer question 2 it is necessary to consider the stage of testing. The testing of individual programs or modules would be done through test data prepared by the programmer. However it would make sense to have a *library* of test data prepared by the systems analyst which would examine all the specified procedures and all the possible data conditions.

It is sometimes possible to use *live test data*. This is often an extract taken from actual data used by the current system. This enables the results to appear more meaningful than that from programmer-produced test data. As such data is usually correct, care must be taken to ensure that error conditions are adequately tested.

The final testing of the system normally takes place after the data files have been converted. This is where the miscellaneous tests listed previously can be undertaken on real, live data.

The use of prototyping in systems development and testing

Prototyping is a technique used by many organizations when it is difficult to determine precisely what the user needs. It is also used where requirements may change during the development process. It is thus systems development based upon *trial and error*, and is therefore a method of *development through continual testing*.

Questions

3 If you were a systems analyst introducing the payroll system, how would you and the user conduct experimental development?
4 List the merits of using a prototyping system.

A point to emphasize is that successful prototyping requires collaboration between the user and you, the systems analyst. In answer to question 3 we can identify the following steps:

1 *Identify the user's basic requirement.* This is normally some form of output. You can then identify the data elements needed to create this output. It is important at this early stage to establish that the requirement can reasonably be met.
2 *Develop the initial prototype.* This is a system that creates the expected output from the data elements. The emphasis here is on *speed and development*. This would suggest the use of a 4GL. It is possible that the processing speed will be poor at this stage, but

that is of no concern yet. It is also likely that the prototype will be incomplete.

3 *Use the prototype to refine the user's requirements.* This step allows the user to get the 'feel' of the system through hands-on experience. This will help the user clarify his or her needs. The user decides what changes are necessary and informs the analyst.

4 *Modify the prototype system* in line with the user's revised requirements.

These last two steps may be repeated several times. The user may try the revised prototype and suggest further changes. The end result will be either the user discarding the system as being inadequate or having the system become operational.

So, to answer question 4, prototyping has several merits as a method of systems development:

1 Different ideas can be tried out quickly and cheaply.
2 A working system can often be delivered more quickly than through conventional means.
3 More meaningful collaboration between user and systems analyst.
4 Effective use of human effort.

There is one important point to watch out for in using prototypes. Sometimes the prototype is incorrectly accepted as the finished article. This may occur despite it being incomplete. For example, it may not be written so as to detect all possible errors and exceptions.

Prototyping is often associated with 4GLs. The reason is quite simple. Third generation languages, such as BASIC and COBOL, were developed before interactive processing through VDUs and relational databases became commonplace. Even with some recent enhancements, they are still relatively ill-suited to on-line processing of information stored in databases. By contrast, 4GLs were specifically developed with these developments in mind.

Using 4GLs

Chapter 6 introduced the concept of 4GLs to you. You could well find your employer using them. Further, as they become more important, and as they are used more often in prototyping, you will need to gain a clearer understanding of them. So we will now say a little bit more about 4GLs.

Question

5 List the qualities of a 4GL and explain why its use facilitates ease of systems development and testing.

Chapter 6 will have provided some clues as to the main advantages of using a 4GL system. Before attempting to answer question 5, we should point out that many experts believe there is no such thing as a fourth generation language. Certainly there is, as yet, no dominant fourth–generation language. What is commonly called a 4GL is really a set of *program development tools*. What the 4GLs have in common is that they are based around the ease of handling one or other of the relational database systems.

Now to answer the question. 4GLs are often claimed to possess the following features:

1 *Improved productivity* as compared with COBOL. This, we would emphasize, relates to *development productivity*, not operation efficiency.

2 *Ease of learning*. It is suggested that a knowledgeable user should be able to make effective use of a 4GL after two days of training. This could help eliminate the problems associated with waiting for programming expertise to solve a simple problem. But whether senior users would want to acquire such skills is another matter. It may also be cost ineffective to have highly paid accountants and marketing experts undertaking a task that can be performed more quickly and effectively by a less highly-paid programmer.

3 *User-friendliness*. Most 4GLs provide a great deal of on-screen help. The help facilities have improved enormously over recent years. Experienced users of the dBASE microcomputer software would certainly contrast the decidedly unfriendly early version, dBASE II, with the more helpful dBASE III Plus.

4 *Close association with a database system*. 4GLs were specifically written with database systems in mind to facilitate ease of access to the organization's central database.

5   *Use of non-procedural code*; in other words their commands are about *what to do*. Third generation languages use procedural code, i.e. *how to do it*. The 'what' is automatically translated into 'how' without programmer or user intervention.

6   *Sensible default assumptions*. 4GL users are often allowed to omit statements, and rely on the systems default assumptions. The help facility provided will often indicate what the default assumption is.

If we widen the scope of 4GLs to include the various programming aids we could make reference to:

1   *Menu generators* which can create a VDU screen menu automatically. All you need to enter are the codes and the corresponding titles.

2   *Program generators*, which translate non-procedural information into a procedural program. Several such generators have been produced over recent years, such as 'The Last One'. This allowed the user to answer a set of standard questions. On the basis of the answers, a program in BASIC was generated.

It would be fair to indicate that 4GLs at present have their limitations. First, they are not capable of being effectively used in all application areas. Secondly, while they may improve programmer productivity, generally they generate less efficient machine code than COBOL. As a result, programs written in 4GLs tend to be slower in operation than their third generation counterparts. Lastly, most 4GLs, though more simple to use than third generation languages, are still complicated for many users. Users therefore do not make a major contribution to programming effort.

Training

The success of a system will depend largely upon the personnel who operate it. This means that a lot depends upon motivation, which is largely in the hands of the organization's management. It will also depend upon *skill*. The purpose of training is to *provide* or *enhance* skills.

Questions

6 You are introducing a new payroll system into the organization, who would you choose for training?

7 For each person, or group of people listed in response to question 6, specify the type of training required.

8 Who would you expect to provide the required training services?

Consider your answer to question 6. There are two groups of people who need to be trained. First, *user personnel*. This seems pretty obvious. Secondly, *systems personnel*. That is to say, the staff who will be operating the equipment will also need to be trained in matters relating to the new system. But do remember that on a small micro-computer-based system the user and the systems person may be, in fact, the same person. Now take a look at your answer to question 7. What are the training needs of user personnel. These can be listed as follows:

1 *Equipment use and troubleshooting.* Users need to be trained to log into the system. They need to know what to enter in order to gain access and what messages the computer will send them. They need to know what to do if the system appears not to function. We have come across cases of user personnel standing by a printer wondering what to do when it had run out of paper!

2 *Application familiarization.* Users may be unfamiliar with the system and need to learn about the role played by the system in the running of the company. A newly transferred sales ledger clerk may not know anything about payroll.

3 *Data capture and coding.* Users need to be trained in the methods of getting hold of the necessary raw data and how to encode it ready for input into the system.

4 *Data handling.* Users must learn how to insert and edit data, and procedures relating to the deletion of data from files. For example, payroll clerks may have to learn that personnel records must not be deleted from the file until the end of the tax year.

5 *Information retrieval.* Users must learn what data they gain access to and how to gain access to it.

6 *Clerical procedures.* User personnel need to know of non-computer

procedures which must be followed. These will include data control and security.

Systems personnel also need to be trained in matters pertaining to the new system. Aspects include:

1 *Equipment usage and troubleshooting.* Some of the equipment may be new or specific to the application. Systems personnel need to know how to handle such equipment and be able to advise users.
2 *Computer run procedures.* Operators need to know about the new programs. What they are called, what resources they require, what reports are produced, and so on. They must learn about timing considerations such as *when* the programs must be run.

Question 8 asks about sources of training and training methods. These could be classified as follows:

1 *Training offered by the equipment supplier.* Manufacturers of large mainframe and minicomputers generally provide training courses on their own premises to their customers. This training is largely 'hands-on' and is often free of charge. The major benefits of users being trained away from their workplace include ability to concentrate on being trained without distractions from the routine of work, and focusing on skills rather than the application of that skill.

   Microcomputer suppliers are far less likely to offer 'free' training. This is partly because the machines are generally sold through retail outlets rather than directly. A further reason is, the low profit margin per machine does not allow for the cost of providing training.
2 *In-house training*, where a trainer provides the service at the customer's premises. The training is then usually tailored to the customer's requirements and specific difficulties can be dealt with. It can also be cheaper to bring one trainer to the company than to have several employees go to the training provider. The main disadvantage is possible distraction of trainees who find the need to go to their offices and thus miss part of the course.
3 *College-based training.* Some colleges provide training in the use of standard pieces of software such as word processors, spreadsheets and database packages. These are usually cheaper than courses provided by commercial training establishments. But until recently, colleges were often unable or unwilling to provide

courses as and when required by clients. Nowadays most colleges and polytechnics, including the Polytechnic of North London, will respond rapidly to requests for training.

4 *Training manuals.* There are many 'teach-yourself' texts and user manuals. Some of them are provided by the software suppliers. While these are able to guide the user through the system, they are at their best when everything goes according to plan. If the equipment or software should present difficulties, or if the trainee were to press the wrong button, there is often nothing that can be referred to to put things right.

Changing over to the new system

The change-over period is the time when the organization changes from the old system to the new.

Question

9 You work for a supermarket chain which has stores all over the country. It has been decided to introduce point-of-sale equipment in its shops. These consist of bar code readers which will read the universal bar code on the product, update the computer records with the sale, print the product description and price on the till roll together with the total owing. What method of change-over from the conventional manual cash till and stock accounting system would you adopt?

The problem posed by question 9 is one faced by many organizations when they introduce a new system. The assumption that we would make is that the system works and is ready to be introduced.

There are three main methods of achieving a change-over to the new system:

1 *Pilot operation.* This is where the system is initially tried out in a few selected stores. The testing will have taken place at head office. While this might have been successful, there is no guarantee that the success would be repeated elsewhere. It is possible that working conditions will be different and the head office simulation was not a valid test.

For our supermarket chain, a pilot operation would probably be a wise choice. First, the damage would be limited if the scheme was unsuccessful. It would be easier to retreat from the system if it were installed in five stores rather than in fifty. Secondly, it would provide the systems analysts with information that might make for easier installation in other branches. Thirdly, it would give other staff, computer operations staff for example, experience in dealing with the system through a gradual build-up. The main problem could be which branches to select as the guinea-pigs.

2 *Parallel running* of the new system alongside the old. It would be a nonsense to try to run two cash tills, one for the old system and the other for the new, at the same check-out point. So this would suggest that parallel running is not a reasonable choice in this case.

So let us consider when it would be sensible. The answer partly is when the customers cannot see that there are two systems operating simultaneously. For example, a stock recording or a payroll system.

The main advantage of parallel running is the added safety. If the new system fails, the organization can revert to the old. There are two main snags associated with this method. First, what happens if the two systems produce different results? How do you decide which is correct? Users may be apt to believe that the old system is correct, despite their previous criticisms of its limitations and failings. Secondly, it is expensive to have two systems doing the same job running alongside one another.

Parallel running is normally limited in time to a number of operating cycles. Often the intention is to have the new system monitor the old for the first cycle. If the results are satisfactory, the new system will come into operation but be monitored by the old for the next cycle. If all is still well, the old system can be dropped.

3 *Direct change-over.* This is where the new system is tested and then adopted without an intervening period of pilot operation or parallel running. This is most commonly found in cases where there is no similarity between the old system and the new.

Such a method is normally the last resort and will follow a period of extensive and intensive testing. The London Stock Exchange system introduced in 1986 was an example of direct change-over, but without the necessary testing. The only proper testing came a week or so before the system was due to go live. Member companies of the Stock Exchange were permitted to test their computer linkages with the new system. During that weekend of testing there were several failures and it was clear that there was going to be a period of difficulty. Nevertheless, the system went live at the duly appointed time, and crashed within an hour!

The Stock Exchange system could therefore be cited as an example of the dangers of direct change-over and how not to introduce a new system.

File conversion

Business computing systems use data files. When a new system is introduced, it will normally use different file structures from the old. What is more, the contents may be slightly different. And not only will the files differ, the hardware might also be different. So, converting existing files into the new format is an important task and may prove to be difficult.

Question

10 How would you convert a payroll system's data files to the format and medium required by the new system?

It is impossible to answer question 10 directly without knowing about the existing system. So let us consider some of the possibilities.

1 *Converting a manual system.* Suppose the present system is based on the use of hand-written paper forms. The way to convert the files is to transcribe the information to disk. This is done either through the use of a key-to-disk system or by direct entry through a VDU keyboard.

There is a number of possible complications. First, the information required for each new record may be stored on two or more different forms. Marrying up the documents may present difficulties. Furthermore, the data entry operators may have to spend a lot of time searching for the particulars required.

Secondly, staff may need to have access to the documents for normal business operations while they are being converted. This conflict of use will almost always have to be resolved when converting manual files.

Thirdly, the converted data records may have to be updated before the new system goes live. For example, suppose it takes longer than a week to convert the data of weekly paid employees. Then the data of the first employees to be converted will be a week out of date. In practice, payroll is unlikely to present major problems of this type because the number of records is normally measured in hundreds and there is an accepted processing cycle. But a sales ledger, by contrast, could present enormous difficulties. Here the number of records could come to several thousand, and any of the records could be updated on any day.

2 *Conversion of computer-held files using the same hardware.* This is a simpler process. For example, one of the authors wrote a payroll system which entailed converting data files from magnetic tape format to disk. This conversion was the result of an upgrade of hardware which enabled data files to be rapidly accessed. It also allowed for various enhancements to the system, such as providing the cost accountant with faster and more accurate information about the wages elements of the overall cost of manufacture.

The exercise required a program to read data records stored in the old format and write output records in the new style. This is a common approach to such conversions.

3 *File conversion using dissimilar hardware.* Where the hardware and file storage media do not allow for conversion by means of a program, things get a bit tricky. One possibility is to print the old file onto paper in a format and sequence that would make data entry easy. Then, you would use the methods as described above for converting manual systems.

Another possibility is that the suppliers of the new hardware may have met this conversion problem before. They may have produced their own solution to the problem of incompatible hardware.

Conversion of live files

This has been mentioned previously. Files in daily use, such as ledgers and stock files, present particular difficulties. Such data files would need to be converted on a specific date. Any amendments from the time of conversion would have to be logged and both the old system and the new updated.

A final requirement is associated with file conversion. That is, to check the new files for both accuracy and completeness. This is normally something that can be done only by the user departments.

Managing the operation of systems development

It will be clear from what we have written in this chapter that implementing a new system involves a great many different steps and operations. It is therefore a huge task, and uses a great deal of the organization's resources, even for a small system. There is a clear need, therefore, for some way of managing the operation.

Questions

11 Who should be in charge of the implementation operation?
12 List the reasons why planning systems development is important.
13 Describe the tools that might be used in planning the implementation process.

There is no simple answer to question 11. A lot depends upon the nature and extent of the new system; whether it affects just one department or several; whether the system is written in-house or whether an applications package is used. We can, however, try to establish some basic principles.

The first thing we can do is distinguish between controlling the overall implementation and the control of the modules that make up the system.

It is common practice, at least for substantial developments, to have a *co-ordinating committee*. This is often chaired by the manager in charge of the department most affected. Others serving on the committee will include the computer manager, the systems analyst in overall charge, and representatives from the other departments affected and the accounts department.

Such a committee, as the name suggests, is concerned with overall co-ordination. It is not necessarily concerned with day-to-day matters. Most of the actual control will be delegated to the systems analyst in charge of the *project team*. Large projects written in-house might even have several project teams working on them. Their work will have to be co-ordinated.

In large organizations, a project team will usually contain a systems analyst and some programmers. In some cases, teams may include a secretary and other staff such as a testing specialist and a documentation expert.

For organizations that rely upon packaged applications software, there may not be any computer specialist project teams. Instead representatives from the user departments and accounts department, and the person in charge of implementation will form their own small project team to monitor progress.

Planning tools

Before looking at the actual tools available to help plan the implementation, let us consider the list you prepared in response to question 12. Perhaps we could start by emphasizing that planning cannot guarantee success, nor does that absence of planning guarantee failure. However, success is more likely if the timings and costings are properly planned.

Planning results in members of the project knowing what is expected of them. That is how many of them are to do the work, when it is start and finish, how much it will cost, etc.

Planning also enables users to know what to expect. That is, when the project will be ready for testing, when it will be ready for implementation, when they will have to do their bit of work, etc.

An absence of planning leaves people without expectations. Poorly planned projects will simply cause disappointment among users. So let us now, in response to question 13, consider some of the planning tools commonly used.

Estimating time requirements

This is a difficult task, depending as it does on the skills and experience of the staff, the complexity of the project, and a multitude of unknown factors.

You might like to think of examples of where you have used this method in everyday life. For example, suppose you were asked to provide an estimate of the time it would take to tidy up a neighbour's garden. If your estimate was accepted, you would be paid £2 for each hour you estimated the job would take. How would you go about making the estimate? The three main methods are:

1 *Historical method*, where timings are based upon what has happened in the past. Consider your providing an estimate for the gardening job, when you may have tidied up that or a similar garden in the past. If you had kept records of the time taken, you would be able to refer to them in preparing your estimate.

    But because it is difficult to make precise comparisons, you may find that this is not a particularly good method. The same is true of estimating times for systems development. The staff may be

	Value	Hours
Grass features: *Average, back & front lawn*	1	
× Length weighting factor (short = .75 Medium = 1.0 Long = 1.3)	1.3	1.3
× Wetness weighting (dry grass = 1.0, wet = 1.1)	1.0	1.3
Shrub features: Per plant	.02	
× plants	30	0.6
Weeding flower beds features: Per 20 m²	.25	
× 65 m²		0.8
Total basic time		2.7
Weather characteristics: × dry: cold 1.1 warm 1.0 hot 1.1 heatwave 1.2 wet: no grass cutting – other activities 1.25	1.1	2.97
Estimated time = 2.97 rounded up to 3 hours		

Figure 8.1   Standard formula for gardening

different, or the projects may have been more or less complex, or the information upon which the estimates are made may be inaccurate.

2 *Intuitive method*, which is nothing better than an educated guess based upon the knowledge and experience of the project leader. Despite its obvious failings it is still the most common method used for estimating timings.

For the gardening job, you would look at the garden and think of a figure and round up to the nearest half-hour or hour. If it is a large garden and you quote a time that is too short, you may get the job but will have to work for more hours for the fixed amount. If your estimated time is longer than the neighbour thinks reasonable you may not be offered the job.

3 *Standard formula method*. This is where a standard formula is used for making timing estimates. You can see the applicability of this idea to the gardening job. You might look at the tools available, the size of the garden, how much is grassed and how much has shrubs, flowers etc., the length of the grass, the weather, etc. Each of these factors will be weighted in your calculations. For example, long grass requires more effort and time than short grass; working in the rain will require more time than if it is dry. Figure 8.1 is an example of a table that you might use to help you make your calculations.

In systems development there are several such formulae in use. One such system suggests the following approximate breakdown of time requirements in systems development:

program design	35%
program coding	35%
testing	25%
documentation	5%

Even here account must be taken of the level of experience of the staff and their personal qualities as well as the complexity of the programs.

Bar charts

Bar charts, also known as *Gantt Charts* after their originator, use bars to indicate the amount of time spent on each task of the systems development program. Figure 8.2 shows a typical Gantt chart. As you

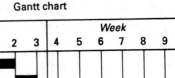

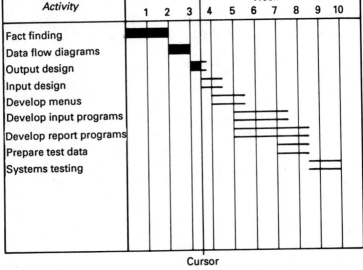

Figure 8.2   Gantt chart

can see, the individual tasks are listed down the left-hand side in the sequence in which they are to be carried out. On the right-hand side is the time information, which goes from left to right.

An open oblong is drawn against tasks for the weeks in which work is to be done on that task. As time passes the oblong is shaded in to show the time spent. Finally, a cursor indicates the current time position.

The benefit of this approach lies in the simple way in which progress can be gauged. Inevitably there are limitations. First, projects with many tasks cannot be easily shown. This can be overcome by sub-dividing the chart. Secondly, the Gantt chart does not show the interrelationships between tasks and how the start of some tasks is dependent upon the completion of others. This can be overcome through the use of PERT charts.

PERT charts

PERT (Program Evaluation and Review Technique) charts also go under the name *network analysis.* The underlying idea is to show the relationships between tasks, that is:

1   Which activities must be completed before starting a specific task.
2   Which activities cannot start until a specific activity is completed.
3   Which activities can proceed in parallel.

Each project is made up of events and activities. An *event* is a milestone or specific objective in the overall scheme, while an *activity* is the application of resources in the task which would enable us to reach the objective. Other information required is the amount of time required for the activity. This enables us to calculate the *float*, or spare time associated with an event. It also enables us to calculate the *critical path*. This is the set of events and activities which do not have any spare time associated with them. We shall say more about this later on.

Figure 8.3 is an example of a PERT chart. Note that there is no relation between the length of the activity line and the time it represents.

Each event is represented by a circle. This contains the event number, together with the earliest time at which the event can be reached and latest time it may be reached. In this example, event four

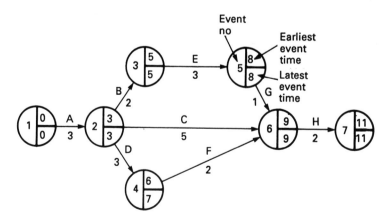

Figure 8.3   PERT chart

is scheduled to be reached no earlier than week six because it takes three weeks to perform activity A and a further three weeks for activity D. Event four could, however, be reached as late as week seven without upsetting things. The reason is that it is followed by activity F which takes two weeks to reach event six. But event six cannot in any case be reached earlier than week nine because of activities B, E and G.

The *critical path* is the route traced through the successive activities that will take the longest time overall. In this case it is activities A, B, E, F, G, H.

Use of PERT charts provides a number of benefits.

1 It requires that the work involved in each activity is carefully examined.
2 It shows relationships between events.
3 It indicates the time required for the job.
4 Examination of the critical path might indicate where resources can be re-allocated in order to eliminate bottlenecks.

However, they cannot record progress and there is no obvious way whereby the current position of the project can be ascertained.

Assignment 8

Find a local business that is introducing a new system. For that new system:
(a) Describe the way in which user staff have been, or are going to be, trained,
(b) Describe the way in which the data files are being converted to the new format, and
(c) Draw either a Gantt chart or a PERT chart of the implementation stages of the systems development.

Recap

Implementation consists of a number of activities; *Testing* is undertaken by both the programmer and the systems analyst. Systems testing is extremely important to ensure that all parts of the system link together correctly. Testing is also designed to ensure that the users gain familiarity with the new system.

A system that involves almost continual testing is *prototyping*. This is where a prototype or experimental system is developed by an analyst and user working together. The end result should be either total rejection of the prototype or acceptance of it as an operational system.

Prototyping usually depends upon the use of 4GL programming systems. While these make for rapid development of business systems, the program code generation is generally slower than that produced by conventional programming means. As a result, systems are often developed using a 4GL, but then rewritten in COBOL or some other third generation language.

Whatever the method of development and source of the system, there is a need to test the *timing* of the system, *backup and recovery procedures*, *peak loading*, and *human procedures*.

Another facet of implementation is the requirement for *training*. Users need to be trained in the use of equipment and in how to carry out the application procedures. Computer personnel also need to become familiar with any new equipment and in the new computer procedures.

Change-over to the new system can be undertaken in three main ways. A *pilot operation* is possible in which the system is implemented in a small part of the organization. Or *parallel running* is possible. This provides added security in case of breakdown, but is expensive in terms of resources because work has to be duplicated. A third choice, best treated as a last resort, is *direct change-over*. Here the old system is switched off and the new one takes over immediately. This is fine if the new system operates without any hitch, but chances are that there will be problems, and direct change-over allows for no fall-back.

Part of the work just prior to, and often during, change-over is *file conversion*. The ease with which data files can be converted to the new format will substantially affect the feasibility of the project. Problems are often faced when trying to convert live files because users need to have access to them and they are often volatile. Similarly, there could be complications when the old and new systems use incompatible file storage media.

The implementation process needs to be managed. This often results in the setting up of a *co-ordinating committee*. It is vital that the user departments are adequately represented in order to ensure that they get the systems they need.

Management implies planning. And there are several planning tools and methods available. Time estimates are important, and formulae are available to help work out how long jobs should take. However, managers still tend to use intuition. *Gantt charts* enable the time dimension to be seen more clearly in the planning operation. They allow progress to be monitored easily. PERT charts do not allow for ease of progress monitoring, but do allow you to see the relationships between the multitude of tasks that make up systems development.

Answers

1 Program testing, system testing, time testing, peak load testing, back-up and recovery testing, human procedure testing.
2 Test data may be programmer-generated. Better to use a library of test data. It is sometimes possible to use live data.
3 The stages are:
   identify the user's basic requirement;
   develop the initial prototype;
   use the prototype to refine the user's requirements;
   modify the prototype as required.
4 Different ideas can be tried out quickly and cheaply.
   A working system can be delivered more quickly than through conventional programming systems.
   There is meaningful collaboration between the user and the analyst.
   Overall, it provides an effective use of human effort.
5 Improved productivity as compared with third generation languages.
   Easier to learn than third generation languages.
   User-friendliness.
   Close association with the database system used by the organization.
   Use of non-procedural code emphasizes *what* is to be achieved, rather than *how* to go about the task.
   Sensible default assumptions.
6 Appropriate user personnel and systems operations personnel.
7 Both groups require training in the use of the equipment and trouble-shooting. Users need to gain familiarity with the application and its method of data capture and entry and how to get information out of the system. They also need to know about relevant non-computer procedures relating to such matters as data control and security. Computer operations personnel need to know about the computer aspects of the system, including what the programs are called, what they are supposed to do, and what media are used.
8 Training could be provided by the equipment supplier or through specialist training organizations.
9 In this case, a pilot scheme would be most appropriate.
10 This depends upon the way in which the data records are currently stored. If they are on paper, then they would have to be key-punched

to disk or entered through the VDU keyboard. If payroll is currently computerized, it may be possible to transfer the data to the new format.

11 This depends on the scale of the project. If it is a large project with several teams working on it, a co-ordinating committee will be required. For a small project, the systems analyst is likely to take charge. However, the managers from relevant user departments need to be members of any implementation committee.

12 It is more likely that the project will run to time and cost. Personnel will know what is expected of them, and when. Users will know what to expect from the system.

13 Time estimating, preferably through a tried and tested formula, Gantt charts and PERT (or network) charts.

9: Selecting business computing hardware and software

Objectives

After reading this chapter, you should be able to:

- Describe how one might decide what size and type of computer to buy
- Outline which features are important in choosing software
- Know where hardware and software can be purchased
- Describe the guidelines to follow in making a final decision.

Scenario

We are back again at Ongar Winemart, the wine and spirit wholesaler, described previously. After graduating with an HND in Business Studies, you have now completed two years with the company. Your talents have been so strongly demonstrated that the managing director (who, coincidentally, is your father) has appointed you as systems manager with responsibility for installing whatever new computer systems the company needs.

The only computer in the company at present is a rather old minicomputer, which is clearly due for scrapping, and is not really up to handling the current workload on the accounts system. You have been told that you can spend up to £100,000 if necessary, but it would be preferable to spend less. How do you set about deciding what hardware and software to buy? What problems lie ahead for you, and what pitfalls do you need to avoid?

Questions

1 Draw up a rough initial shopping list for Ongar Winemart, of things that might be bought from the £100,000 computer budget. There is no need to be too precise about requirements, or to worry about prices at this stage.
2 What should you do now?

From a position of almost total ignorance, our shopping-list for question 1 might look something like this:

- Multi-user computer with several terminals
- Several microcomputers
- Networking hardware and software
- System software
- Accounting software for main computer
- Other applications software for main computer
- Various microcomputer packages.

Regarding question 2, the most important thing is to seek advice, and to be prepared to listen to that advice. Advice is available from various sources:

- *Within the company*: accounting staff know the current system well, both its strengths and its weakness
- *Computer salesmen*: these represent a useful source of free advice, so long as you keep them at arm's length
- *Computer consultant*: even if their advice is expensive, it will still be much cheaper than paying for your own mistakes.

The first stage in the process is to carry out a systems investigation, as described in Chapter 4. This would probably include interviewing all staff who are likely to use the new computer, in order to determine requirements and draw up a more precise specification. If you really are inexperienced, then it would be wise to get help from a consultant on organizing the interviews, possibly even getting the consultant to do many of the interviews.

The major decision is deciding what hardware and software to buy for the main accounting system. Any decisions about buying microcomputers and other software are less critical, and probably will not affect the major decision. Networking might restrict your choice of supplier, because you might have to be satisfied that the supplier was competent to install any networking needed, as well as the main computer.

Sizing the computer

At first sight, it may seem an insuperable technical problem to decide what size and type of computer you need. In fact, it is not that difficult. After all, people manage to buy motor cars without knowing what happens under the bonnet. They are usually also capable of realizing that if they have a family of twelve children, then they need a minibus rather than a car. How do they find out what decisions to make? By reading magazines and talking to other car users, who already own the sort of car they are interested in. The same ideas need to be applied in buying a computer.

There is little difficulty in choosing a suitable single-user microcomputer, so we shall assume you are buying a multi-user system. The first obvious step is to decide how many users need to be supported at a time. Remember that there may actually be more users in the company than can be supported at a time, because some may be only occasional users. The volume of printing needed is also important, in order to specify what type of printer is required. An accounts system will usually require a relatively fast dot matrix printer, because of the large volumes of printing needed. This decision may affect the choice of computer, because a small computer may not be able to drive the volumes of printing required.

Once you have decided how many users you need and the speed of printer, you can set about drawing up a 'long list' of possible computers and suppliers. As we mentioned in Chapter 2, there are three other main considerations in sizing a computer:

1 *Disk capacity*. How much permanent storage is needed?
2 *Memory*. How much RAM do you need?
3 *Processor*. Is it powerful enough to support the system?

Even in the early 1980s, disk capacity and RAM were still a major consideration for systems analysts in specifying a system. This is no longer the case, as both have become very cheap.

Disk capacity

In fact, it is not difficult to calculate how much space is needed for your accounts system. Software suppliers will give you formulae which calculate how much space is needed, given a specified number of customers, stock items, invoices per customer per day, and so on. For example, one might need to allow 500 bytes per customer, plus some fixed overheads for the file; plus, of course, the stock file, the supplier file and all the various transaction files. Even so, a moderately large accounts system such as Ongar Winemart is most unlikely to take up more than 10 MB of disk for data files. Space will also be needed on disk for the operating system, the accounts software and any other necessary software. This software might require another 10 MB or so, making a total of 20 MB or so.

This requirement has to be set against what is now generally available. Hard disks have become very cheap, and a 70 MB disk would generally be regarded as the minimum for a multi-user system. For the Ongar Winemart system, assuming eight or ten users, one would probably specify a 150 MB or even a 300 MB disk. This may seem excessive, but it adds very little to the cost, and it is quite surprising how disk space does get used up over a period of time.

It is also very important to look at the average *access time* for a disk. In processing accounts, much of the work is concerned with reading and updating disk files; fast disk access is crucial in achieving good performance.

RAM

This is not usually significant in buying a computer, as one simply takes the manufacturer's recommendation as to how much RAM is needed for a given number of users. It is now common for single-user micros to have 4MB of RAM, but an operating system like OS/2 needs a lot of RAM, and each user on a multi-user computer with a less sophisticated operating system would probably need rather less RAM. The large memories on microcomputers also reflect the fact that the software like Lotus 1-2-3 can be expensive on RAM.

Nevertheless, one would expect at least 256 KB per user on a current multi-user system, and often much more is available. Just as with disk, there are no great savings to be made by cutting down on the amount of RAM.

Processor

The potential performance is difficult to assess, and yet very important. An overworked processor can provide very slow responses to users, which is irritating and also costs money. Many multi-user systems use the UNIX operating system and one of the standard processor chips, which makes it possible for an experienced analyst to make a reasonable estimate of performance. On the other hand, minicomputer manufacturers often use their own proprietary processor chips, which may be very good, but may be more difficult to assess.

In any case, the performance of the processor is not the only factor. Performance is affected by other aspects of the computer design, and most especially by the speed of the disk access.

Question

3 Ongar Winemart are scrapping their old computer because of irritations with the current system. List some of the problems that might have bothered them.

If you talk to any company with an old accounts system, they will probably give you a long list of irritations. Some of these will relate to lack of capacity, associated with obsolete hardware and with an accounts system which has outgrown its original specifications. Others will relate to unfriendly software, because it used to be accepted that computers were difficult to use. With the arrival of 'user-friendly' software on microcomputers, this is no longer acceptable and software on minicomputers and mainframes has been redesigned to be much easier to use. This means that old software can now sometimes appear very unfriendly and old-fashioned.

Without actually knowing Ongar Winemart, one can only cite a few typical problems in response to question 3. Your list is probably quite different from ours. Our list, based on experiences of various users we have met, is as follows:

● Lack of disk space, meaning that only very limited invoice details are accessible, so that it is difficult to answer customer queries about unpaid invoices

- Very poor response from computer, often having to wait minutes for simple requests, making it hopeless to deal with telephone queries
- Software which requires the operator to remember quite unmemorable customer and stock codes, and provides no 'help' system
- Lack of adequate checks on input, so that input data errors remain, which could have been eliminated at an early stage
- Poor correction procedures on data input, so that when a mistake is made, a whole screenful of data has to be re-typed.

Assessing computer performance

There are three objective ways of assessing whether this is adequate: by using benchmarks, by running hardware simulations or by running your own tests.

1 *Benchmark* tests involve running standard programs which are designed to test various facets of computer performance. They are commonly included by computer magazines in reviews of new microcomputers. They generally provide a useful guide in assessing the relative performance of different microcomputers, but are of much less use when it comes to assessing multi-user systems.

2 *Hardware simulations* are provided by some manufacturers; these are computer programs which evaluate the operation of a particular hardware configuration under specified workloads. They can give a reasonable guide as to whether a particular processor can cope in the specified situation, but precise workloads are always difficult to predict. Simulations are probably most useful for a large organization which intends buying a complex hardware system with several processors.

3 *Running your own tests*: this can involve running programs of your own (for assessing hardware) or using test data (for assessing software). While a good idea in principle, it is extremely difficult and time-consuming to set up effective tests in practice. Unless you have a very large budget, suppliers are unlikely to co-operate for long in such tests, for fear of making a loss on the deal. Such tests are usually only carried out for major companies making a decision on a very large purchase.

The major problem is that it is not really hardware performance that bothers the average user, but the speed of response as they perceive it. This relates to various pieces of software, as well as hardware. Any objective tests are of limited value, because they can never precisely emulate the live situation.

The best solution for most prospective purchasers is to make a relatively subjective assessment. Reviews in computer magazines can often be useful, but the best means of assessment is to talk to current users. If they manage to support a workload similar to yours, then the computer will probably do what you need.

IBM computers and compatibles

IBM have totally dominated the microcomputer market ever since they launched their first microcomputer, the IBM PC, in 1982; the later IBM AT has been equally successful (AT stands for 'advanced technology'). There are now many different makes of '*IBM-compatibles*' (also referred to as '*IBM clones*') on the market; many of these are made in Taiwan or elsewhere in the Far East. Sometimes, these machines are described as 'PC-compatible' or 'AT-compatible' to emphasize the set of specifications to which they conform. Generally, it is sensible to buy clones, because they provide the same or better performance than IBM microcomputers at a lower price. You do have to take care with some of the more obscure makes because they may be unreliable, and have poor servicing, or they may even infringe IBM patents. You also have to be careful that an IBM-compatible is genuinely compatible; some software that runs on IBM microcomputers does not run on all compatibles, especially software that is very graphics orientated.

In 1987, IBM launched the PS/2 series, which will no doubt be just as successful as previous IBM microcomputers. It has better specifications, and offers improved performance, although many users (such as Ongar Winemart) will find the power offered by ATs and AT-compatibles to be as much as they can possibly use. The major benefit offered by the PS/2 series is likely to be the graphics operating system, Presentation Manager, which will be available with the Microsoft OS/2 operating system. This will enable the operating system to be more user-friendly, and will also allow *multitasking* by the operating system i.e. several programs can be loaded into memory at the same time, and the user can switch between them.

The PS/2 is designed with improved internal communications technology, known as *multi-channel architecture (MCA)*. This is designed in such a way that it will be very difficult to 'clone'. Nevertheless, 'PS/2-compatibles' will no doubt appear eventually.

Question

4 Why do you think Ongar Winemart might justify buying some microcomputers as well as their main computer?
List some possible uses for these micros.
5 What need do Ongar Winemart have for networking? Is it likely to be justified?

For question 4, you should be able to give a long list of possible benefits. Use of microcomputers has mushroomed in most companies, regardless of what other computers are available and even when the data processing department disapproves. These are some of the points we would list in response to question 4:

1 Microcomputers are now very cheap. A computer with software can be bought for less than £1000, which is less than a month's wages for most staff. Even very small time savings, or slightly improved information, will justify the expenditure.

2 Microcomputer software is generally much better and cheaper than the same software on minicomputers. It therefore makes sense to analyse data on a micro, especially as using a package such as Lotus 1-2-3 is easy and gives great flexibility in producing reports.

3 Microcomputers give the user total independence. You will not be slowed up by poor response, and you can switch on the micro whenever you wish, or even take it home at weekends.

Likely uses have been indicated earlier in the book, especially in Chapter 7. Some possibilities are:

● Word processing, for reports and correspondence
● Mailing list: use of database software to do selective mailings of customers and prospective customers

- Sales analysis and financial projections: use of spreadsheets to analyse market research data and outputs from the main accounts system
- Smaller databases e.g. for keeping a record of customer queries and complaints
- Personnel records system.

Regarding question 5, some of the applications listed will run totally independently of other computers. Since networking adds considerably to the cost of a microcomputer, it may be better to keep it as a 'stand-alone' machine where this is feasible. Networking between various microcomputers will be justified, where data needs to be passed frequently between the various users, or where they need to share expensive peripherals such as laser printers.

Where the microcomputer user needs to take data from the main accounts system, it will save a deal of time if the microcomputer can be directly connected to the main computer. A direct connection means extra cost, but this will easily be justified, on one or both of the following two arguments:

1   Without a connection to the main computer, data will have to be printed out by the main computer, and keyed back into the microcomputer. This is frustrating, as well as being a total waste of money, and happens in all too many companies.
2   Where the user needs both a terminal to the main computer, and a microcomputer for other work, then it is cheaper and more convenient to use a microcomputer for both functions.

Paying for the computer

There are two ways of purchasing a computer:

1   Buying outright.
2   Paying in instalments or renting.

As you might expect, it is cheaper to buy outright but this will not be sensible if the business is short of cash. Where large sums are being expended, computer dealers will arrange leasing deals through finance houses with varying degrees of complexity, rather similar to a normal hire purchase agreement. For a small multi-user system, the hardware and software will usually be purchased outright, but the finance provided by a leasing deal.

For mainframes and large minicomputers, the hardware can be bought for cash or on a leasing deal; large manufacturers such as IBM often offer rental deals. Systems software is usually got from the same source as the hardware, and often can only be rented. Applications software is usually obtained separately, and may be bought outright, but often is rented from the supplier.

The payments do not end if hardware and software are bought outright. A maintenance deal is necessary on hardware to ensure that breakdowns are rapidly dealt with by engineers. Software houses also require a maintenance contract on large packages, as a condition of issuing you with the regular updates to the software. With microcomputer software, maintenance contracts are less usual, but you will have to pay for any software updates.

Question

6 How should Ongar Winemart choose their software? What distinguishes good software from bad software?

If Ongar Winemart were just buying microcomputer software, then the second part of question 6 could be fairly easy to answer. Most microcomputer software has been on the market for several years; if a package has survived for that length of time, and is still in popular use, then it is probably very good. If there is any doubt, it is always wise to talk to current users of the package, before making a decision.

However, it is not enough for software to be good and well designed; it also needs to be appropriate for Ongar Winemart if it is to be any good for them. They need to identify their needs clearly, because different packages are designed for different users. The next section spells out in more detail what they might be looking for.

Selecting software

Here, we first consider criteria for standard packages such as word processing, spreadsheets, database and utilities. Afterwards, we consider applications software.

Standard microcomputer packages

Here, it is difficult to go badly wrong, because there is so much good software available. Packages are sufficiently cheap that you can usually afford to discard them if you discover after a while that they do not quite do what you want. Some criteria that you may find useful are:

1   *What help messages are provided?*
These need to be clear and ideally should be 'context-sensitive' i.e. help messages should relate to the particular command that you are about to give.

2   *Is the manual clear, and is it necessary?*
Forget the software, if a manual is needed often, unless the software has some fairly unique features. You only need a manual if the help facilities are bad.

However, a good, clear manual is useful. You will probably need to scan through it initially to familiarize yourself, and you will occasionally need to check out particular features.

3   *What facilities are available, and does the package include all the facilities that you need?*
This is obviously crucial, and a reasonable indication is given by publicity material produced by software companies. The best guide is probably the reviews published in microcomputer magazines, and especially the comparisons that they publish regularly of different packages.

4   *What type of user is the package aimed at?*
For example, some word processing software has a wide range of facilities, and is designed to provide a powerful tool for professional journalists and secretaries. Other packages are less sophisticated, but easier to use for casual users. You need to find software which is pitched at the right level for you.

5   *Is the software 'menu-driven' or 'command-driven'?*
This distinction applies especially to database packages, but applies to some other software. Menu-driven packages such as Reflex are usually simpler to use, but less powerful than command-driven software such as dBASE3. A command-driven package can be customized for a particular application, which is then very easy to run.

6   *How long does the package take to learn?*
We normally allow a maximum of thirty minutes to gain an initial

understanding of a new standard package, unless it has something very special to offer. If it takes any longer, we abandon it. An inexperienced user perhaps ought to allow three or four hours, with a little bit of help from a more experienced user.

If a package is too complicated to use, it is probably not worth bothering with. You will not only spend too long learning to use it, but if you come back to it after a couple of months, you will then have to spend time re-learning it.

The general rule in choosing software is to keep things as simple as possible. However, where staff are skilled at using computer software, it may be appropriate for them to use more sophisticated packages such as dBASE3 in order to design simpler systems for others to use.

The final point is that standardization is essential. For example, there is not much to choose between Lotus 1-2-3 and Supercalc; what matters is for a company to fix on one package, and thus to avoid problems of incompatibility.

Standard minicomputer/mainframe packages

There are many packages on larger computers such as database packages and decision support systems which are similar to the microcomputer packages just discussed, but generally far more sophisticated in what they offer. The points already mentioned regarding microcomputer software need to be considered, and security features are also likely to be a major consideration. Assessment is far more difficult because:

1 Reviews, if available, tend to be superficial and not very useful.
2 Larger companies are totally unstandardized, and therefore different versions of software need to be developed for different machines. This means that, for example, a Prime version may not be available and the ICL version may be less 'user-friendly' than the IBM version.
3 Performance of the software may be important, if it is to be used for heavy 'number-crunching'.
4 The package is likely to have a wide range of facilities, and it will require considerable effort to evaluate these.

Any company buying such software is likely to have considerable 'in-house' expertise, otherwise they will not be in a position to make effective use of the software. Even so, it is often worth seeking advice from consultants, since the cost of such software is likely to be from £20,000 to £100,000.

Fortunately, most software houses will allow prospective customers to have the software for a period of evaluation. This allows them to assess the software both in terms of suitability and in terms of performance.

Applications software

The points mentioned in relation to standard packages again apply, although the help facilities are often less developed. In fact, sophisticated help facilities are perhaps less useful for applications such as accounting, because the software is menu-driven and is used for a limited number of fairly standardized tasks. A clear, concise manual is essential, because many of the tasks performed by an applications package will need more explanation than can be provided by help messages.

Two points are particularly important in choosing applications software:

1 *Draw up a detailed specification first*
   Unless you have a detailed specification of the system you require, you cannot be sure that the applications package does what you need. Preferably, find a package that will do more than you need, and give you scope for further developments of your system in the future.
2 *Careful attention to security and control*
   For many applications, especially accounting, a package is useless unless it has an adequate system of passwords and an adequate audit trail.

Where can you buy computers?

Before we answer this question, it is best to consider the main types of businesses involved in selling computers:

1 *Dealers* sell direct to customers from offices or even from high street shops. Generally, they sell microcomputer hardware and software, although some larger dealers may sell networks or small

multi-user systems. Often, the larger and more specialist dealerships will be held by computer consultancies.

2   *Distributors* are the 'middlemen' in selling microcomputers. They will be responsible for distribution to a large dealer network, and may also sell direct to some very large customers.

3   *Hardware manufacturers* design and assemble computers, often from parts made elsewhere in the world. Microcomputers are usually sold via distributors and dealers, although some manufacturers sell direct. Larger computers are often sold direct. Manufacturers of large computers often develop software for their own computers.

4   *Software houses* develop and market their own packages. These may be sold direct, or via dealers, or via hardware manufacturers.

5   *Computer consultancies* offer advice on purchase of hardware and software. They will usually carry out systems analysis for clients, and specify and write bespoke software for them. They often sell applications software which they have developed. They may also hold dealerships for hardware and other suppliers' software.

Buying microcomputers and small minicomputers

These will be bought through dealers. The main thing is to buy your computer, printer and software through the same dealer, unless you really know what you are doing. This may be slightly more expensive, but it does avoid the situation of not being able to tie down responsibility for problems.

Particular care is needed in choosing the right dealer if you are buying a network, or software for applications such as accounting. Large companies such as Pegasus Software Ltd have set up their own network of licensed software, precisely because they have recognized the need for adequate expertise in selling their software.

Some smaller manufacturers of multi-user systems prefer to sell directly to customers, but larger manufacturers generally sell through dealers. There are also certain microcomputer manufacturers who sell direct, usually selling IBM 'clones' assembled in the Far East. These offer very cheap deals, but you do need to know what you are doing.

Buying minicomputers

The medium range of minicomputers, supporting up to about sixty users, is usually sold by computer consultancies who hold dealerships.

They are intended principally for applications such as accounting. The dealer would typically offer a range of applications software to run on the computer, claiming to offer a total solution to a user's business information problems.

Buying large minicomputers and mainframes

These computers are usually sold by manufacturers, designed to meet a customer's specific requirements. Some systems software is sold by manufacturers, while applications software is usually bought from software houses. Mainframe contracts may run into several million pounds, and are characterized by very long and detailed specification documents, with customers having very considerable computer expertise.

Rules to follow in making a decision

This last section is a brief summary of the rules to follow in buying computer hardware and software. Some important DOs and DON'Ts are:

1 DO choose software, rather than hardware.
2 DO buy all hardware and software from one dealer where possible, unless you are very confident of what you are doing.
3 DON'T buy software just because a dealer says it is good. Make sure you understand before you buy, even if you do need to ask boring, niggling questions.
4 DO get as much advice as possible.
5 DON'T sign a contract until you have sorted out all your major queries. Dealers are always more available for advice before you sign a contract.
6 DO make a clear decision when you have found out what you need to know. DON'T let it happen by default, because a dealer is pressing you.
7 DO draw up a clear cost justification before deciding to purchase either software or hardware.

If you are unsure of what you are doing, independent advice is available from various sources, and need not be very expensive. The Association of Independent Computer Consultants (AICC) can give you a list of consultants. Alternatively, most polytechnics (including the Polytechnic of North London) offer an advice service.

The sensible steps in arriving at a final decision are likely to be, in rough sequence:

1 Visit other users first.
2 Arrange demonstrations of several different systems.
3 Select the system which best fits your information needs.
4 Ensure the dealer is knowledgeable and reliable.
5 Draw up a detailed list of costs.
6 List the benefits.
7 Decide whether the computer is worth buying.
8 Define job responsibilities.
9 Draw up a schedule for implementation and training.

Thus, buying computer hardware and software is not too difficult. If you follow the rules we have laid down, and use a reasonable degree of common sense, you will be surprised how easy it all is. People are far more difficult to manage than computers, but that is another story altogether.

Recap

Choosing the *size* and *type* of computers to buy is simply a question of estimating the number of users on the main computer, and the number of additional microcomputers required. To support a specified system requires adequate *RAM*, *disk space*, and *processing* power.

Microcomputers are usually worth buying even in addition to a minicomputer because of the benefits, including use of 'user-friendly' software and independence from the main computer. The cost of *networking* is justified where microcomputers need to communicate with one another, or with the main computer.

IBM-compatibles offer a cheaper and often equally good alternative to IBM–AT microcomputers. The *IBM PS/2* series of microcomputers are becoming increasingly popular.

Selecting *standard microcomputer packages* is just a matter of selecting popular software which meets your requirements. Magazine reviews are very useful for this. Selecting *standard mainframe software* is more difficult, and it may be useful to get the software on an evaluation period.

In selecting *applications software*, great care is needed to ensure that the software meets your requirements. For *accounting software*, security and control features are most important.

Answers

1 Multi-user computer with several terminals;
   several microcomputers;
   networking hardware and software;
   system software;
   accounting software for main computer;
   other applications software for main computer;
   various microcomputer packages.
2 Seek advice; carry out a systems investigation.
3 Lack of disk space;
   poor response from old computer;
   unfriendly software;
   poor input data checks, causing errors to be picked up later;
   inefficient input data correction procedures.
4 Microcomputers are cheap;
   software is better and cheaper than on minicomputers;
   micros give the user independence.
5 Where data needs multi-user access e.g. accounting;
   where peripherals need to be shared;
   where data needs to be passed between a micro and the main computer, or where a micro can double up as a terminal to the main computer.
6 Decide whether it is user-friendly enough, and whether it meets their requirements (see text for further details, this question does require a fairly long answer).

References

1 Carter R. *Students' Guide to Information Technology*. Oxford: Heinemann Newnes, 1989.
2 Carter R. *Students' Guide to Office Automation*. Oxford: Heinemann Newnes, 1989.
3 Senn J. A. *Analysis and Design of Informative Systems*. McGraw-Hill, 1986.
4 Bradley J. *Data Base Management in Business* 2nd edn. Holt, Rinehart and Winston, 1987.
5 Roberts N. *Using dBASEIII on the Amstrad PC* Oxford: Heinemann, 1988.
6 Byers R. A. *Everyman's Data Base Primer with dBASE3* Ashton-Tate, 1986.
7 Waller D. *Book-Keeping with Pegasus* Paradigm, 1987.
8 Jenkins B., Perry R., Cooke P. *An Audit Approach to Computers* Chartac (ICAEW), 1986.

Index

Accounting 41, 47, 121, 126, 131, 149–172, 183, 208, 220
Analyst Programmer 37
ANSI 130, 133
Applications Software 35, 120, 149–183, 198, 217, 220–222
Artificial Intelligence 143
Assembly Language 129, 147
AT-compatible 214
Audit Trail 173, 220
AutoCad 179

Back-up 176
Balance Sheet 16, 166
BASIC 130–132, 147, 189, 191
Batches 119
Benchmarks 213, 215
Bespoke Software 37, 176, 221, 141
Binary 129
Bursters 104
Business 1–19, 131, 132, 147

Cacheing 34
CAD 179
Change-over 171, 194–5
Clones 214, 221
COBOL 131–133, 135–137, 139, 147, 189–191
Command-driven 218

Commercial language 132
Compatibles 214
Confidentiality 172
Contract accounting 170
Communications Network 42–5, 177
Compiler, 129, 130
Computer-Aided Design (CAD) 30, 179–180
Computer-Aided Manufacture (CAM) 30
Controls 117, 172, 193
Critical Path 204
Cylinder 115

Database 34, 38, 41, 43, 44, 117, 137–143, 153, 181, 190, 215, 216, 217
Database Management System (DBMS) 117
Data Dictionary 92–5, 117
Data Flow Diagrams 87–94, 117
Data General 132
Data Preparation 47
Data Protection Act 172
dBASE III 117, 140–143, 147, 181, 190, 218, 219
Decollators 104
Dealers 220
Desktop Publishing (DTP) 179–180

Direct Access Storage Device (DASD) 114
Direct change-over 195
Disk 31, 114, 127, 172–174, 197, 210
  fixed-head 115
  floppy 114
  Winchester 114

Economic Order Quantity (EOQ) 162
Electronic Mail 17, 177
Electronic Office 178
Ethernet 43
Exchangeable Disk Pack 114
Expert System 143, 146

Fact Finding 61–2, 77–86
  interviewing 77–81, 211
  observation 84–5
  questionnaires 82–3
  record inspection 86
FCS-EPS 179
Feasibility 45, 63–5
Field 32, 112
File 32, 110, 112, 114, 121, 157–9, 175, 192, 196
  archival 113
  back-up 113
  conversion 172, 196
  indexed sequential (ISAM) 116
  log 119
  master 112–113
  organization 111, 115–116
  reference 111–113
  relative 116
  report 113
  sequential 116
  spooler 113

transactions 113
Financial Planning 178
Fire 118, 175
Flooding 118, 175
Flowchart 127
Focus 138
Fortran 130–1, 135–6, 147
Fortress Plus 174
Fourth Generation Language (4GL) 37–8, 117, 130, 134–140, 147, 152, 189–91

Gantt Charts 201–2
Graphics 179–80, 214
Guillotines 104

Hackers 118, 173
Hardware 31, 114, 136, 170, 175, 196–7
  hardware simulation 213
Harvard Presentation Graphics 179
High-level language 130

IBM 35, 43, 214, 219, 132
IBM-compatible 35, 43, 214, 221
ICL 219
Implementation 223, 171
Index 137, 142
Information Systems 14–8, 24–30, 52–8
Ingres 138
Input Design 108–111
Input Validation 110–111
Integrated accounting 150–152
Interpreter 130
Invoicing 156, 157
ISAM 116
ISSCO Graphics 179

Keyboard 31, 127, 174, 196

Leasing 216
Ledger
  Nominal 16, 150, 152, 164,
    166, 169, 173
  Purchase 15, 150, 152, 164,
    169
  Sales 15, 37, 76, 150, 152, 153,
    157, 169, 171, 173, 197
Lisp 146
Local Area Network (LAN) 42–
  3
Lotus 1-2-3 41, 174, 178, 211,
  215, 219

Macro-program 140, 144
Mainframe 41, 113, 126, 130,
  132, 138, 147, 151, 152, 170,
  179, 193, 212, 217
Management Control 28
Management Information 28
Manpower Planning 180–1
McCormack and Dodge 150
Memory 31
Microcomputer 31, 41–5, 113–4,
  116, 118, 130, 132, 140, 147,
  150, 174–5, 177, 179–80,
  192–3, 210, 212, 214–7, 221
Micro-FCS 179
Microsoft 35, 131, 214
Microsoft Chart 179
Minicomputer 40, 113, 132, 138,
  147, 150, 177, 179, 193, 212,
  217, 221
MSA 150
MS-DOS 35, 131
Multichannel Architecture
  (MCA) 215
Multitasking 214

Multi-User Systems 35, 40, 173,
  212, 221

Network 42–3, 177, 210, 215–6,
  220
Network Analysis 203
Nominal ledger 166–168
Norton Utilities 175
Novell 43

Omicron 150, 152, 166–7
On-line 119
Operating Systems 35, 211
Operations Requirements 14
Operators 47, 193, 195
Oracle 138
Organization Charts 70–2
OS/2 35, 131, 214

Packaged Software 34, 37, 61,
  120–1, 132, 150–2, 176, 199,
  218–220
Parallel Running 195
Pascal 132, 135
Passwords 118, 173–4, 220
Payroll 15, 36, 38, 120–1, 150,
  168–9, 181, 185, 187, 192,
  195, 197
Pegasus 150, 154, 157, 161, 163,
  165, 221
Personnel 180–1, 216
PERT Charts 203
Pilot Operation 194
Portable 129
Power Supply 118
Primary Sector 2, 4
Prime 219

Printer 31, 104, 179, 192, 210, 221
Procedural 134–5, 191
Processor 202, 204
Profit & Loss Account 15, 166
Programmer 36, 46, 136, 185–6, 199
Programming 126, 141
Programs 34–5, 46–7, 59, 118, 121, 134, 185–6
Prolog 146
Prototyping 59, 61, 188–9
PS/2 214–5
Purchase ledger 164

RAM 31, 212
Random Access 116
Record 112, 142
Record Key 111–3, 116
Reflex 218
Relational Models 117
Re-order Level 162–3
Robocad 179
ROM 31

Sagesoft 150–2
Sales Ledger 153
SAS Graphics 179
Scientific Languages 130
Screen 31, 111, 178
Secondary Sector 3–4
Security 117–9, 172, 193, 220
Sequential Access 116
Shrinkage 27, 55, 162–3
Single-User Systems 174, 210, 211
Software 31, 34–5, 59–61, 114, 118, 126, 136, 160, 170, 174–5, 178, 180, 182–3, 210, 217–220

Software House 38, 217, 220–1
Source Code 130
Specification 220
SPSS 181
Spreadsheets 34, 118, 178–80, 182, 216
Stock control 161–164
Structured programming 136
Structured Query Language (SQL) 138
Supercalc 178, 219
Syntax 127, 130
Systems Analysis 35–6, 46, 61–2, 195, 221
Systems Design 61–2, 100–122
Systems Development 58–61, 198–199
Systems Requirements 59, 73–6
Systems Software 34

Tailored Software 37, 39
Tape, magnetic 113
Tape Streamers 114
Technicians 47
Telecom Gold 177
Terminals 43, 177, 182, 216
Tertiary Sector 3–4
Testing 61, 185–7
Third generation language 130, 189
Token Ring 43
Torus 43
Training 122, 136, 171, 191–4
Transaction 26, 153, 173, 178, 186
Turn-Round Document 105, 109

Unix 35, 132, 212
Updating 26

User-Friendly 37, 134, 152, 212
User Manuals 122, 192
User Requirements 59, 100, 190,
    212, 214
Utility Software 34, 217

Validation 110–111, 119

VDU 40, 105–7, 111, 187, 191,
    196
Wang Office System 177
Word Processing 34, 142, 176,
    180, 215, 217–8
Wordstar 174, 177
Workstation 179